# Legacy of Laughter

*a treasury of Newfoundland wit and humour*

## Jack Fitzgerald

# Other Jack Fitzgerald books

*Newfoundland Adventures – In Air, On Land, At Sea*
*Ten Steps to the Gallows – True Stories of Newfoundland and Labrador*
*Treasure Island Revisited – A True Newfoundland Adventure Story*
*Newfoundland Disasters*
*Untold Stories of Newfoundland*
*Ghosts and Oddities*
*A Day at the Races – The Story of the St. John's Regatta*
*Beyond the Grave*
*Jack Fitzgerald's Notebook*
*Beyond Belief*
*The Hangman is Never Late*
*Another Time, Another Place*
*Where Angels Fear To Tread*
*Newfoundland Fireside Stories*
*Strange but True Newfoundland Stories*
*Amazing Newfoundland Stories*
*Up the Pond*
*Stroke of Champions*
*Too Many Parties, Too Many Pals*
*Convicted*
*Rogues and Branding Irons*

Ask your favourite bookstore or order directly from the publisher.

Creative Book Publishing
P.O. Box 1815
367 Water Street
St. John's, NL
A1C 5P9

Tel: (709) 579-1312
Fax: (709) 579-6511
E-mail: nl.books@transcontinental.ca
www.creativebookpublishing.ca

Please add $5.00 Canadian for shipping and handling and taxes on single book orders and $1.00 for each additional book.

# Legacy of Laughter
*a treasury of Newfoundland wit and humour*

## Jack Fitzgerald

St. John's, Newfoundland and Labrador
2007

© 2007, Jack Fitzgerald

We gratefully acknowledge the financial support of The Canada Council for the Arts, The Government of Canada through the Book Publishing Industry Development Program (BPIDP), and the Government of Newfoundland and Labrador through the Department of Tourism, Culture and Recreation for our publishing program.

All rights reserved. No part of this work covered by the copyrights hereon may be reproduced or used in any form or by any means — graphic, electronic or mechanical — without the prior written permission of the publisher. Any requests for photocopying, recording, taping or information storage and retrieval systems of any part of this book shall be directed in writing to the Canadian Reprography Collective, One Yonge Street, Suite 1900, Toronto, Ontario M5E 1E5.

Cover design by Maurice Fitzgerald
Layout by Todd Manning
Printed on acid-free paper

Published by
CREATIVE PUBLISHERS
an imprint of CREATIVE BOOK PUBLISHING
a division of Transcontinental Media
P.O. Box 1815, Stn. C, St. John's, Newfoundland and Labrador A1C 5P9

First Edition
Printed in Canada by:
TRANSCONTINENTAL PRINT

Library and Archives Canada Cataloguing in Publication

Fitzgerald, Jack, 1945-
    Legacy of laughter / Jack Fitzgerald.

ISBN 978-1-897174-16-6

    1. Canadian wit and humor (English)--Newfoundland and Labrador.
2. Newfoundland and Labrador--Anecdotes. I. Title.

PN6178.C3F58 2007        C818'.602        C2007-903716-X

# Dedication

*I am pleased to dedicate this book to the late Fred Adams, a Newfoundland author whose love for old St. John's was contagious. Fred, who along with being a walking encyclopedia on old-time St. John's, was a wonderful story teller and it was always a pleasure to spend time with him.*

# Acknowledgements

*While researching and gathering stories for this book and in getting it to publication, I was pleased to have the help and support of the following people: Don Morgan, Bob Rumsey, Donna Francis, Maurice Fitzgerald, the staff at the City of St. John's Archives, the staff at the Newfoundland Collection of the Hunter Library, the staff at the Centre of Newfoundland Studies, MUN; Mike Critch, Richard 'Dick' Hartery, Brian Healy, Jack Murphy, Pat Hearn, Jim Casey, Frank and Jean Murphy, John Hamilton, Helen Miller, Neachel Keeping and Bill Bennett.*

# Table of Contents

| | | |
|---|---|---|
| Chapter 1 | Mickey Quinn and Contemporaries | 1 |
| Chapter 2 | Wit and Humour from the 1940s | 61 |
| Chapter 3 | From the 1950s and 1960s | 105 |
| Chapter 4 | From the 1890s and 1930s | 159 |
| Chapter 5 | From 1725 to 1890 | 205 |

# Chapter 1

# Mickey Quinn and Contemporaries

If you go to the Delta Hotel on the corner of New Gower Street and Barter's Hill, you might not know that before the Delta was built there was another, much smaller hotel on the site. It was called the Brownsdale Hotel, and in those days, before the Barter's Hill realignment, it was on the corner of New Gower Street and Brazil Square. The Brownsdale was popular with outport merchants and sea captains when they had to stay in town to do business, and their lesser contemporaries stayed in a variety of boarding houses in that area.

If you enter the Delta, you just might go to Mickey Quinn's to have a snack, or a beer, to shoot a game of pool, or to try your luck on the one-armed bandits. What you might not know is that Mickey Quinn was a real person, a resident of that warren of narrow streets and small houses that covered the area up to the late 1950's and early 1960's.

Mickey was one of the numerous characters of old St. John's, who were quite capable of doing a day's work when the opportunity presented itself, and who were also capable of not showing up if something more interesting came up. By the time you finish reading this chapter, you will know things about Mickey Quinn that history has long forgotten. This chapter contains the largest collection of Mickey Quinn stories ever published. Most of them really happened, and those that didn't, should have.

## The Yule Log and Mickey Quinn

In 1902, Mickey Quinn was living on the lower part of Pleasant Street. One Christmas Eve, a neighbour, Mrs. Evans, looked out the window and commented to her husband, "Look, Bill, the Quinn's are bringing in a Yule Log."

"Yule log, my arse! That's Quinn," said Bill.

## Quinn the Store Clerk

Mickey Quinn and his brother Jack were helping Mrs. Lawlor in her grocery store on Duckworth Street. A customer was inspecting the eggs on display. She picked up one and asked Mickey, "Are these eggs strictly fresh?"

Mickey asked Jack, "Feel the eggs, Jack, and see if they're cool enough to sell yet?"

## The Ham Sandwich

Mickey and Jack Quinn were walking out Logy Bay Road after a visit to Sugar Loaf Pond one May 24$^{th}$ weekend. Broke and hungry, Mickey said, "Just think, Jack, if I had a big fat slice of ham, I'd have a ham sandwich, if I only had two slices of bread."

## Mickey and the Army

Mickey Quinn boarded the train at Brigus Junction and took a seat in the smoking lounge which was filled with members of the Newfoundland Regiment returning to St. John's from out of town manoeuvres. As the afternoon wore on, song and story went the rounds, and old battles were fought anew when Mickey struck in:

"Gentlemen, to look at me you would not credit the experiences I have been through, but I think the most thrilling of all was when, several years ago, I stood and confronted, single-handed, a desperate crowd who thirsted for my blood. Alone I braved them, when suddenly a shell whistled through the air and burst right in my face."

Captain J. O'Grady of the Regiment scrutinized the countenance of the meek looking Quinn and commented, "It certainly isn't much of a face, but, at the same time, it doesn't look as though a shell burst in it. What regiment were you in?"

"I never said I was in a regiment," drawled Quinn. "It was an egg shell. I'm an actor." Which, at times, he was!

### Quinn met Religious Obligation!

At a time when Roman Catholics were forbidden to eat meat on Friday, Mickey Quinn found himself in a Water Street Restaurant wanting to eat meat, but bothered by the fact that it was on a Friday. To do so would result in the commission of a mortal sin. Yet, if no alternative was available, there would be no sin. Mickey asked the waiter, "Do you have any stewed whale?"

"No, we don't," answered the waiter.

"Do you have any fried sharks or boiled penguin?" asked Mickey.

"No sharks or penguins, Mickey," replied the waiter.

"Okay," said Mickey Quinn, "in that case, bring me a beefsteak smothered with onions and gravy. The Good Lord knows I asked for fish."

### Supper with Mickey and Danielle

Mickey Quinn was having supper with Professor Danielle at his Royal Pavilion[1] on the banks of Quidi Vidi Lake. Professor Danielle had gone through one of his eloquent lofty spiels with Mickey listening attentively. Finally, he picked up a serving dish on the table and, placing it in front of Mickey, commented, "Said Aristotle unto Plato, have another baked potato?"

Ignoring the offer and reaching out for the bottle of wine on the table, Mickey answered, "Said Plato unto Aristotle, thank you, I prefer the bottle."

### The Literary Mickey Quinn

Mickey Quinn and his brother Jack were guests at supper with the eccentric Professor Charles Danielle. In his usual manner, the

---

1. The Royal Pavilion was a splendid hotel and restaurant built by the Professor at Quidi Vidi Lake and opened to the public on Regatta Day 1893.

Professor had some fun with the Quinns. To test Jack Quinn's literary knowledge, he asked, "Do you like Omar Khayyam?"

"Well, I like Omar Khayyam a little, but I prefer Chianti!" replied Jack.

Mickey noticed that the Professor struggled to conceal his laughter. While walking home, Mickey told his brother, "Why, in the Lord's name don't you simply say you don't know when you're asked something you don't understand? Didn't you see that smirk on the Professor's face when you said you preferred Chianti? Omar Khayyam is not a wine, you idiot! It's a brand of cheese."

## Dinner Protocol at the Royal Pavilion

While helping to prepare a dinner meeting at Professor Danielle's Royal Pavilion, the cook was concerned about the formalities. The Professor called his employees together to plan the dinner. Among them was Mickey Quinn. During the discussion the cook asked, "How do I announce dinner when it's ready? Should I say, 'Dinner is ready or dinner is served?'"

Mickey spoke up, "If it's like it was yesterday just say dinner is burnt!"

## The Professional

Word got around the Plymouth Road neighborhood in St. John's that a man who claimed to be a *Diesel Fitter* had moved into a boarding house on Brewery Lane.[2] *Slacker* Baird, *Little Dickie* Gray, *Dead Eye* Murphy and Mickey Quinn were hanging around at the Furness Withy Wharf in the east end and the topic of conversation was the Diesel Fitter who just moved into the neighborhood. None of them seemed to know exactly what it was that a Diesel Fitter did. Mickey said he could explain. He told his friends that the man worked at Ayre's Department Store, and whenever he noticed a husband pointing out that knickers "ladies underwear" were on sale, he would pick up a pair and tell the man *Diesel Fitter!*

---

2. Brewery Lane is known today as Cook's Lane off Plymouth Road.

### Bottle in Hand

Constable Fitzgerald met Mickey Quinn in front of the post office on Water Street and said, "Mickey, every time I see you; you got a bottle in your hand."

"Yeah, well I can't keep it in me mouth all day," snapped Quinn.

### The Earliest Mickey Quinn Story

The wit of Mickey Quinn was displayed at an early age. His older brother Jack delighted in telling this story about his brother when Mickey was just five years old. Mrs. Quinn had been invited to a friend's house for afternoon tea and decided to take Mickey with her. She had a real task to convince him to leave his friends for his mother's social visit. Mrs. Quinn put Mickey in the tub and gave him a good-scrubbing, then put on his Sunday best outfit. All the while, she was telling him the delights he could expect at the *tea*.

"There will be chocolate cake, pies, buns, and maybe even some ice cream," she told him. After arriving at their destination, Mickey sat quietly on a chair in the parlour and never opened his mouth. Finally, the host stood up and said, "Well, it's time to have tea. Will little Mickey help us?"

"Well, dat's what we came for, wasn't it?" an irritated Mickey quipped.

### Ate Too Much

Mickey ate too much chocolate cake. He clutched his stomach and groaned.

"Are you in pain?" asked his mother.

"Naw!" said Mickey. "The pain is in me."

### The Quinn Etiquette

When Mickey returned home from tea at his mother's friend's, his father asked him if he enjoyed himself. He said, "Oh Pop! I do love cake. It's awful good."

His mother told him, "Mickey, you should not say *love* cake, say *like*. Do not say *awful*, say *very*. Do not say *nice* say *good* and by the way, the word *oh* should be left out. Now see if you can repeat the sentence correctly."

"I like cake. It's very good," stated Mickey.

"That is better," his mother said.

Mickey said in disgust, "Yeah! But it sounds like I'm talkin' about bread."

### Mickey's Dog

Mickey Quinn's mother sent him to Aylward's Store on New Gower Street to purchase a gallon of potatoes.[3] He was gone a long while and Mrs. Quinn became worried. She looked out the window and saw Mickey coming up the street with a rope tied around a dog's neck and dragging the dog who resisted him at every step with all four legs. When he got home with the dog at the end of the rope, he asked his mother, "Can I keep the dog, he followed me home."

### Mickey and his brother Jack Quinn

When the Quinn brothers were growing up, Jack was not as kind to little Mickey as he ought to have been. He tried hard to shake him off so that he might go and play with older boys, but Mickey managed to keep up with him.

"You should be ashamed to treat your little brother in that way," Jack's father told him, "little Mickey should be sacred to you."

Jack respected and feared his dad and made no comment. He went out to play with his friends and Mickey rushed to follow along. Jack waited until they were out of sight of their father and he addressed Mickey, "Always taggin' along after me! If you weren't so sacred, I'd blacken yer two f——n eyes."

### Mickey and Jack at school

Mickey and Jack Quinn were late for school. To avoid detention, they concocted a story that Mickey had been bitten by a dog,

---

3. In those days and well into Confederation, potatoes were measured from the bin in a gallon bucket.

and Jack stopped to help him. The principal at St. Patrick's Boys' School surprised them by asking to see the bite. Mickey pulled up the leg of his pants, and the Principal said, "Sure, there's no bite marks there!"

Quick as a wink, Mickey Quinn said, "The dog had no teeth, Brother. C'mon Jack, we better get to our class."

### Jack Quinn Understands Oxygen

While the Christian Brother was explaining to his class how oxygen affects human beings, Jack Quinn was doodling on the cover of his exercise book. The brother noticed Quinn's lack of attention and he asked, "Jack, what would happen if there was too much oxygen in the air?"

Without hesitation, Jack answered, "We would all blow up and burst."

### Quinn as a Youth

Mickey's brother Jack liked to tell of the time the Christian Brother asked Mickey to use a sentence with *antidote* in it? Mickey gave it some thought, then answered, "Me Uncle Paddy loves me, but me *antidotes* on me."

When asked to write two sentences, one with the word *arrears* in it and the other with the word *butter*, Mickey wrote, "My brother Jack and I both have to wash in back of *arrears*."

And for *butter*, he wrote, "She wanted to go to the dance, *butter* mother wouldn't let her."

On a similar test he was asked to construct a sentence using the word *Amazon*. Mickey wrote, "You can pay for the eggs, but the *Amazon* me."

His brother Jack also showed promise as a wit in school. He was asked to write two sentences, one with the word *Income*, the other using the word *Folder*.

He wrote: "I opened the door and *income* the cat." And, "Children should always show respect *folder* people."

### Mickey's Paragraph on Nutrition

The teacher assigned the class the task of writing a paragraph about nutrition. Mickey Quinn wrote:

Our bodies need all kinds of hot stuff such as hot dinners and all other kinds of stuff to build the body for if our bodies didn't get any food we would drop down for want of hunger.

### Mickey Defines the Nose

In a general science assignment, Mickey defined the nose this way. "The nose is divided into two parts, the inner ear and the outer ear. You have to blow it often to keep it clean."

### Sweetheart Left Quinn

Mickey Quinn was broken hearted when his first childhood sweetheart left him for a fella from the west end of the city. With pen in hand, Mickey wrote a song describing his innermost feelings. The words to that song are long forgotten, but the title is remembered. That title was, "If I can't be your number one, then number two on you."

### Mickey Quinn goes to Boston

Legend has it that, while in his late teens, Mickey Quinn went to Boston where he married a Newfoundland girl and stayed a few years before returning to live in Newfoundland. While strolling along a downtown Boston Street, Mickey stopped at a large fruit store to admire the splendid array of fruit in the window. He was impressed by a grapefruit which was the largest he had ever seen. Mickey asked a couple of Bostonians standing nearby, "What makes the fruit grow so big in this country?"

"Why climate, of course!" one replied.

"Oh," commented Mickey and he joined the two people in walking along the street, engaged in conversation. When they entered a block of recently built skyscrapers, Mickey asked, "What makes the buildings so high in his country?"

The smart-ass answered, "Why climate, of course."

Mickey was not pleased with the reply and decided it was time to give as good as he got! He asked the two people, "Do you know that we have a tower, the Cabot Tower, at St. John's, Newfoundland that signals all the ships entering the harbour, and it's seven hundred and fifty feet above sea-level?"

"Good gracious," said the Bostonians, "and how in blazes do you get up that?"

"Why," says Mickey Quinn, "climb it (climate) and be damned!"

## Quinn Cheating Customs

When Mickey Quinn returned to Newfoundland from Boston, he carried a bottle of liquor with him which he had purchased at a low price, but had to be declared to Customs upon entering Newfoundland and a tariff paid. Quinn felt he could slip one by the Customs. He carefully concealed the bottle among his clothing inside a rather large suitcase, and hoped that officials would not search it. When he arrived at St. John's, he was asked by a Customs Officer what he had in his valise.

"Nothing but old clothes," replied Quinn.

"Are you sure there's nothing but old clothes?" asked the official.

"That's all, nothing but old clothes, hardly worth looking at," answered Quinn.

To Quinn's surprise, the official opened the valise "suitcase" and probing inside it, pulled out a bottle of Canadian rum. "I thought you said you had nothing but old clothes," exclaimed the officer.

"Sure, that's what I said," said Quinn.

"But what do you call this?" said the official as he held up the bottle of rum.

"Oh, that, that's my nightcap!" exclaimed Quinn.

## What Jack thought of Mickey

Jack Quinn told his brother Mickey, "You know, Mickey, I think the world of you."

"I do, and I know what you think of the world!" commented Mickey.

### The Screens

When Mickey Quinn first visited Professor Danielle's farm overlooking Quidi Vidi Lake, he was impressed by the screened doors and the screened windows. He asked, "Are there many mosquitoes around here?"

"None! Absolutely none!" answered the Professor. "I installed the screens to keep out the flying fish!"

### Diligent Workers

Professor Danielle to Mickey and Jack Quinn at Danielle's farm, "What are you two doing?"

"We're carrying these boards over to that lumber pile," replied Mickey.

"Where are the boards?" the Professor asked.

"Jasus, Jack, we forgot the boards," said Mickey.

### Quinn Quoting Bible

"Always remember that quote from the Bible: 'Don't worry – here comes the quilt!'" exclaimed Mickey Quinn to Professor Danielle.

"You got that wrong, Mickey. It should be, 'Fear not – the comforter cometh!'"

### In Step with the Judge

Mickey Quinn, while filling in one summer as a cab driver in St. John's, became involved with an argument with a customer that led to fisticuffs. When he appeared in court, Judge Knight asked, "What's your occupation, Mr. Quinn?"

"I'm a cab driver, yer honour," answered Quinn.

"You mean you are the driver of the horses attached thereto," said Judge Knight.

"Yes, sir," said Quinn.

"You are charged with hitting this man on the face. Did you do it?" asked Judge Knight.

"No, yer honour," stated Quinn.

"What did you do, then?" asked Judge Knight.

"I busted him on the nasal organ attached thereto," replied Quinn.

### The Quinn Brothers

The Quinn brothers, Mickey and Jack, were helping Jack Rossley paint the interior of the Star Hall on Henry Street in preparation for its transformation into the Rossley Star Theatre in 1911. Jack was on a ladder painting the ceiling in the stage area. Mickey asked Jack, "Have you got a good grip on your brush?"

"I do." says Jack. "Why?"

"Well, hold it tight, I'm taking away the ladder," answered Mickey.

### Quinn and Billy Devan, the Vaudeville Star!

Mickey Quinn was chatting with Billy Devan, a famous Vaudeville performer from New York, who was rehearsing at the Rossley Vaudeville Theatre on Henry Street where Mickey sometimes worked and sometimes participated in plays. The topic turned to tracing ancestors and Devan asked Quinn if he had ever traced his ancestors. Quinn told Devan, "Oh, yes, I can trace my ancestors back to, to well, I don't know exactly who, but we've been descending for centuries."

### Devan Pays Tribute to Quinn

Billy Devan was so popular with St. John's theatre goers that his stay in the city was extended three times. He had developed a good friendship with Quinn and on his last night was delivering a stand up comedy routine. Mickey, seated in the front row, occasionally tossed a barb at Devan, who turned it to his own advantage and had the audience roaring with laughter. When it came time to bid his final farewell, he said, "It's been wonderful, coming all the way from New York to co-star on stage with Mickey Quinn." Quinn's stature as a town character grew tremendously that night.

### At the Rossley Vaudeville Theatre - Henry Street

Mickey Quinn was in the audience at the Rossley Theatre during a variety show, which included a magician's performance. It wasn't a great performance at all. When the magician turned to the audience and asked, "Can anyone loan me an egg?"

Mickey shouted. "If I had one, you'd have it before this."

### Mickey Quinn's One Act Play

Mickey sometimes performed on stage at the Rossley "Star" Theatre on Henry Street. The story was told of a short skit he wrote, and in which he performed.

**Scene:** Overseas. Nfld. Regiment Barracks.

**Characters:** Two soldiers, Private Mickey Quinn and Private *Dead-eye* Murphy.

**Quinn:** Got a pen I can borrow?
**Dead-eye:** Sure thing, pal.
**Quinn:** Got some paper?
**Dead-eye:** Anything for a pal!
**Quinn:** Are you going past the mail-box when you go out?
**Dead-eye:** Sure am, old-buddy.
**Quinn:** Wait till I finish this letter.
**Dead-eye:** Not a problem, friend.
**Quinn:** Lend me a stamp.
**Dead-eye:** Certainly!
**Quinn:** What is your girlfriend's address?

### *Buffalo Bill* and Quinn at the Rossley

During May 1913, the Rossley Theatre featured a Cowboy Act called *Buffalo Bill* with Vaudeville comedian Joe Burkhardt as *Buffalo Bill*. Jack Rossley also performed in the Act.

There was a scene on stage where Burkhardt, as *Buffalo Bill* and Rossley, his sidekick, are resting at a campsite along a river adjoining Indian Territory. Mickey Quinn was given a small off-stage part in the act with only five words, which left the audience howling.

While *Buffalo Bill* and his sidekick rested, the sound of Indian drums could be heard in the distance. *Buffalo Bill* turned to his sidekick and in a concerned voice said, "I don't like the sound of those drums."

Mickey, on the other side of the river and off-stage shouts, "He's not our regular drummer."

Next day the *Evening Telegram* described the *Buffalo Bill* Act as, "one of the finest acts ever staged. The hall was so crowded that a great many had to go away disappointed at not being able to get in. It is the greatest comedy and funniest of all the acts ever seen here."

### Good Voice

After a rehearsal at the Rossley Theatre, Mickey Quinn asked Jack Rossley, "Do ya think I will ever be able to do anything with my voice?"

Rossley answered, "It might come in handy in case of fire."

### Matty Hearn at the Rossley

Matty Hearn, a regular member of the audience at Rossley's Star Theatre in St. John's was seen leaving the hall during the interval of one of Jack Rossley's new comedy plays.

Mickey Quinn, the doorman, asked, "What's the matter, Matty, don't you like the show?"

"It's not that, Mickey," answered Matty. "It's just that the program says the second act takes place two weeks later and I promised the Misses I'd be home by midnight."

### Quinn Outwits Jack Rossley

Jack Rossley once loaned some money to Mickey Quinn. A long time passed and Quinn had made no effort to repay the loan. Rossley, a shrewd businessman, thought he would use a little psychology on Quinn.

One day in front of the Queen's Theatre off Water Street, he stopped Mickey and said, "Look here, Quinn, you seemed to have forgotten about the money I loaned you. I'll tell you what I'll do. I know times are tough, so I am willing to meet you half-way and forget about half of it."

"In that case," says Quinn, "I'll meet you half-way and forget about the other half."

As Rossley walked away shaking his head, he was heard to say, "The first hundred jeers are the hardest."

### Billy Devan Curious

After befriending Mickey Quinn at the Rossley, Billy Devan asked him, "How well do you know Slacker Baird?"

"Why, I know him very well," replied Quinn.

"Well, Mickey, he's looking for a few days work. Can a person believe what he says?" asked Devan.

"Yes and no. It has been my experience that if he tells you the truth, you can believe every word of it, but brother, if he lies to you, you'd better have no faith in him at all," replied Mickey Quinn.

### Not New to City

Billy Devan: "Is St. John's a healthy place to live?"

Mickey Quinn: "Yes, boy, it is. When I arrived in St. John's, I couldn't walk or eat solid food."

Billy Devan: "What was wrong with you?"

Mickey Quinn: "Not a thing – I was born here."

### No Trumpets Please!

When Mickey Quinn first went to work at the Rossley's Star Theatre, part of his job required him to work off-stage moving props. During a performance at which the Star was filled to capacity, there were several scenes in which the orchestra in front of the stage would stop playing and a solo trumpeter would play from off-stage. When the performers arrived at the time for the first solo to be played, there was nothing but silence. Rossley signaled to the orchestra to cover the silent time and the play moved on. Then it came time for the second off-stage solo and there was no trumpeter. An angry Jack Rossley rushed to the off-stage area to see why the trumpeter was not playing. He found Mickey Quinn with one arm holding the trumpeter in a head-lock.

"What in God's name are you doing, Mickey? There's a live performance going on," Rossley said angrily.

"I told him that and warned him that he can't play the trumpet back here, but he won't listen," explained Mickey.

### Count Me Out!

At a time when Jack Rossley was taking his show on the road to an outport community, he offered Mickey Quinn ten dollars to join the group and participate in the show. By this time, Mickey had been around the Rossley Theatre long enough to know how show people bicker over salary. He told Rossley, "You can double that or count me out!"

"One, two, three, four, five, six, seven, eight, nine, ten.... and you're out!" replied Rossley.

### Quinn the Lawyer

Mickey Quinn insisted on defending himself in a court trial. He took the stand to tell his side of the story.

Prosecutor: "You say you went to the home of Mrs. Murphy?"

Quinn: "And that I did, sir!"

Prosecutor: "Now, Mr. Quinn, will you please tell the court exactly what Mrs. Murphy said to you."

Quinn: "Your Honour, I object to the question!"

A legal wrangle followed among the Judge, Quinn and the Prosecutor that lasted more than an hour. Mickey fought tooth and nail to prevent the question from being asked.

Finally, the Judge said, "Proceed, Mr. Prosecutor, I see no reason as to why the question cannot be asked."

Prosecutor: (displaying a satisfying grin) "Now, Mr. Quinn, as I was saying...tell me exactly what Mrs. Murphy said to you."

Quinn: "She said nothing. She wasn't home!"

### Good Looking?

Waitress to Mickey Quinn: "Don't you think I'm rather good looking?"

Mickey: "In a way."

Waitress: "In what way?"

Mickey: "A way off."

### Tried to Forget

Mickey Quinn went missing for several months during 1907. When he showed up again at his boarding home at Dogs Town in the east end of St. John's, neighbours and friends gathered around and asked where he had been?

Mickey explained, "I just got fed up with life in the city, so I went to Harbour Grace to forget St. John's. Then I went to Trepassey to forget Harbour Grace."

### Quinn in St. Paddy's Day Parade!

Mickey Quinn, *after drowning the shamrock*, marched down Water Street with the Benevolent Irish Society in the 1909 St. Paddy's Day Parade. Instead of turning left at McBride's Hill, he turned right and ended up in the St. John's Harbour. It was the only water he touched all day.

St. Paddy's Day is the holiday when the Irish march over LeMarchant Road and stagger down Water Street singing, "I'll take you home again Kathleen, because all that screech has turned you green!"

### Drinks to Keep Steady

Mickey Quinn: "Don't you think Slacker drinks an awful lot?"

Dead-eye Murphy: "I dunno, Mickey, he tells me he only drinks to steady himself."

Mickey Quinn: "Well, I just left him at Victoria Park and he's so steady, he can't move."

### At Sir Edgar's Mansion

Mickey Quinn was called to Sir Edgar Bowring's mansion on Forest Road to repair a gas-leak in the parlour. The maid warned Mickey, "You better be very careful of the floors. They have just been polished."

"Don't worry, ma'am," said Mickey, "there's no danger of me slippin' on your floors. I have spikes in me shoes."

### Trouters

Mickey Quinn is trouting at Silver Springs, now part of the Rennie's River System in St. John's. Judge Prowse walks by with a pole in his hand, looking for a good spot to wet a line. He asks, "Are the fish biting today?"

"Well, if they are, yer honour, they're only biting each other," answered Mickey.

### Loan 'til Payday!

Mickey Quinn approached Johnny Duff (who in later years operated the Queen's Theatre and York Theatre) and asked, "Johnny, my friend, can you loan me five dollars 'til payday?"

"And when is payday?" asked Johnny.

"How do I know, you're the one who's working," replied Mickey

### Quinn on the Express

Mickey Quinn rushed excitedly into the smoking car of the Newfoundland Express and shouted, "A lady has passed out in the next car! Has anybody got a shot of whiskey?" Instantly, three men each pulled out a flask and offered it to Quinn. Taking the nearest one, Quinn guzzled a long drink and as he handed it back said, "Thank you, sir. It always makes me sick to my stomach to see a lady faint."

### Mickey Quinn in a Barrel!

At a time when Mickey Quinn was down on his luck, he took up sleeping in a molasses barrel down on Bowring's Wharf. He had settled away in his barrel home one night and lit up a cigarette and was puffing away. He had a good view of Water Street from the bung-hole of the puncheon which faced Water Street.[4] Constable Churchill was passing by and saw the flame made by the match when Mickey lit his cigarette. He went down to the barrel and flashed his light through the bunghole and asked, "Who's in there?"

---

4. The bunghole of a puncheon was the hole in which a tap was inserted to drain the molasses from the puncheon or barrel as it was also called.

Mickey responded, "Get away from the window and come around to the door."

### Quinn the Waiter

Mickey Quinn worked as a waiter for a few months in a Duckworth Street Restaurant which claimed it could supply any dish ordered. A visitor to St. John's asked Quinn for a Polar Bear sandwich? Mickey was up to the occasion and answered, "Sorry, sir, we're all out of bread!"

"I'd like a dinner with two pork chops, and make them lean!" said the customer.

"Lean on which side, sir?" Mickey asked.

### Quinn at Dobbin's

Once, while eating a dinner at Dobbin's Restaurant on Duckworth Street, near Market House Square, Mickey Quinn asked the waiter, "How was this steak cooked?"

"Smothered in onions, Mr. Quinn," answered the waiter.

"Well, it died a hard death," snapped Quinn.

### Quinn and the cook

After finishing a bowl of soup at Dobbin's Restaurant, Mickey addressed the cook, "You say you served with our troops in France?"

"Yes, Mickey, I was cook for two years and was wounded twice," replied the veteran.

"You are a lucky man," said Quinn. "It's a wonder they didn't kill you."

### Another visit to Dobbin's

During another visit to Dobbin's Restaurant, Mickey Quinn had been left waiting a long while for his meal.

"Hey, Waiter!" he shouted.

"What is it?" the waiter answered.

"Well, what I originally came in for was breakfast, but if dinner is ready now, I'll take supper," said Quinn.

### Quinn and the Butcher

Mickey goes into Lawlor's Butcher Store in the east end of St. John's and asks Mr. Lawlor, "If I can leave security with you, which is equal to what I take away, will you trust me until next week?"

"Not a problem, Mickey!" Lawlor answered.

Mickey: "In that case, give me two of your hams and keep one of 'em until I come back next week."

### Quinn and the Doctor

The doctor told Mickey Quinn that if he did not give up alcohol, it would shorten his life. "Think so?" Quinn asked.

"Certainly. If you stop drinking, I am confident it will prolong your days."

"I think you're right," Quinn commented. "I went twenty-four hours without a drink a few months ago, and I never put in such a long day in my life."

### Quinn in Court

Around 1910, Mickey Quinn and Corker Tibbs, both well-known characters of the time, were brought up before the Judge of the Central District Court and charged with being drunk and disorderly on the public street. The first to be called was Tibbs. The judge said to him, "You're charged with being drunk on the public street. What do you say to that?"

"Guilty, your honour," admitted Tibbs.

"Where do you live?" the judge asked.

"Nowhere. I have no home," replied Tibbs.

Quinn was then called to the bar and charged with his offense. He, too, pleaded guilty and the judge asked, "Where do you live?"

Replied Quinn, "Next door to Tibbs, your honour."

(This same story was also told with Quinn's friend Joey Baird).

### Three Little Bears

The boarding mistress was reading the story of the three little bears to her two small children. "Poppa Bear said, 'Who's been eating my porridge?'"

Mickey Quinn spoke up and said, "See children, we are not the only ones that got cockroaches."

### Quinn's Boots

Mickey Quinn wrote his son in Boston suggesting that he come home. Mickey wrote that times were tough and his son would be better off at home in St. John's with family and friends. Young Quinn wrote back that he had a job and was doing very well and intended on remaining in Boston. Mickey gave some thought to his son's reply then sent another letter. In this letter, he said his boots were in bad shape and he couldn't afford to buy a new pair, and suggested that since his son was doing well, he send his father a new pair of boots. Young Quinn did as his father requested then hung the boots on a telegraph line with his father's name and address attached. Later that day, a hobo came along and took down the boots, tried them on and finding they were a perfect fit, he kept them. He left his old boots on the telegraph wire. Several days later, young Quinn came by and noticed the old boots on the telegraph line replacing the new ones he thought he had wired to his father. He turned to a friend with him and said, "Dad must have got the boots I sent him, and he sent me back his old ones."

### The Logic of Quinn

At the Regatta of 1904, Mickey Quinn was approached by a German seaman, who was there to watch his buddies race against the local naval reserve, and asked if he could speak German.

"Not a word," says Quinn, "but my cousin's husband can play the German flute."

### The Devil is a Landlord

Two Englishmen, who were visiting St. John's, encountered Mickey Quinn walking along Duckworth Street. Pointing up Prescott Street, one of them asked Quinn, "Listen 'ere old chap, what do the locals call that hill?"

"The Devil's Stairway," answered Quinn.

Then pointing towards Water Street, the second Englishmen asked, "What do you chaps call the street below here?"

"We call that the Devil's Promenade," Quinn answered.

"Well then, the Devil seems to own a lot of property around here," chuckled the Englishman.

"In dat he does. In dat he does. Sure the Devil is an absentee landlord living over there in England," Quinn commented as he went on his way up Duckworth Street.

### Quinn Hated Holidays

Mickey and his brother Jack were standing at the corner of Water Street and McBride's Hill on St. Paddy's Day, a national holiday in Newfoundland.

"I hate holidays," commented Jack Quinn.

"Yes, it makes you feel common when nobody else is working," added Mickey.

### The Silver-Tongued Quinn

On another occasion, when Mickey was down on his luck, he stood outside Baird's Store on Water Street East, begging. A prominent lady of St. John's, when approached by Quinn for a few coppers, asked, "Why should a grown, healthy looking man like you be begging?"

"My lady, it is the only profession I know in which a gentleman can address a beautiful woman without an introduction," answered Quinn.

The lady gave him a contribution that financed the rest of his day.

### The Extravagant Quinn

A few days passed and Mickey found himself in a similar situation. He stopped a lady to ask for a hand-out.

"I'm almost famished. Can you help me?" Mickey asked.

"Here's five cents. But how did you fall so low?"

"I had your fault, Madam. I was too extravagant," quipped Mickey.

## Quinn Dining Out

On another occasion, while going door to door begging on Waterford Bridge Road, Mickey asked the lady of the house if she could provide him with something to eat. Leaving Quinn standing at her front door, she went to the kitchen and returned with a bag containing some food and said, "Here, you can eat this outside, if you don't mind."

"If I don't mind?"

"Yes, that's what I said."

"Well, bless you, ma'am, I don't mind. I'm used to it. When I was at home and in clover as it were, it was me daily custom, when donnin' me dress suit, to announce to me butler, "Parkins, don't await dinner fer me tonight. I'm dinin' out.""

## Quinn and the Hypnotist

Mickey was minding the office at the Rossley while Jack Rossley was doing business uptown. A man entered the building and stopped to talk to the security man. "Where's the manager's office? I am a performer looking for a job?"

"You're not a bloody hypnotist, are ya?" asked the ticket man.

"No, sir, I am not," answered the performer.

"Then go up to the second floor, turn right and go on down the hall."

At the top of the stairs, he was met by the cleaning woman. "Where's the manager's office," he asked.

"You're not a damn hypnotist, are ya?" asked the woman.

"No, I'm not," replied the man.

She told him to go to the end of the hall and take the door on his right. The man entered the manager's office and was met by Mickey Quinn. Quinn explained that Rossley was out, but that he could make an afternoon appointment for him. The man was pleased to make such an arrangement. But before writing down the appointment, Mickey asked, "By the way, your not a hypnotist are ya?"

"Everyone I've met since I entered this building has asked the same question. What's the big problem with hypnotists?" he asked Quinn.

"Well, it's like this. Two weeks ago Jack had a hypnotist in his show. The hypnotist was great. Everybody loved his act. Then he hypnotized the entire audience," explained Quinn.

"Wow!" said the stranger, impressed by what he was hearing.

"Then," Mickey continued, "when he moved towards the front of the stage, he struck his foot on a stage light and shouted, "Shit!" Well, we're still cleaning out the theatre," concluded Quinn.

### Jack Quinn

Jack Quinn was said to be every bit as witty as his brother Mickey. After asking a lady coming out of Baird's Store on Water Street for a few cents, she told him, "You seem able-bodied and healthy. You should be strong enough to work!"

Jack replied, "True enough, ma'am. And you seem beautiful enough to be in the movies, but its obvious you prefer the simple life."

### Begging on Circular Road

Mickey stopped at the Circular Road home of a well-known St. John's family where he had been fortunate over previous weeks. The lady of the house was irritated and in a hurry. She asked Quinn what he wanted this time, and told him to answer as precisely and as quickly as he could.

Mickey inhaled a deep breath and said, "Will you, madam, give me a drink of water because I'm so hungry, I don't know where to stay tonight?"

### Quinn Arrested

Mickey was bold enough to drop into the court house lockup one day and ask the desk Sergeant for the price of a cup of tea. The policeman asked, "Quinn, do you ever work?"

"Now and then," said Quinn.

"What do you do?" asked the policeman.

"This and that," replied Quinn.

"Where?" asked the officer.

"Oh, here and there," said Quinn.

The officer, deciding to have some fun, seized Quinn by the arm and said, "I'm locking you up for panhandling." He locked Quinn in a cell.

"When will I get out of here?" Quinn asked.

"Sooner or later," answered the officer.

### Quinn and Slacker

Mickey Quinn and a bunch of his friends went to Mount Pearl for a picnic during the summer of 1909. When Slacker Baird discovered that Mickey had eaten his sandwich, he challenged Mickey to a fight. Quinn turned and ran with Slacker in pursuit. Quinn ran into a wooded area and seemed to have disappeared. Slacker Baird searched the woods and found himself in the middle of Maloney's Meadow. He stopped when he realized he was in a large puddle of cow dung. At this time, Quinn came out from behind a tree, and seeing Slacker's predicament, shouted to the others, "Help! Help! Slacker is melting."

### At Casey's Farm

Shortly after the first steamroller was introduced to St. John's, it was seen going across Casey's Farm, near to where St. Clare's Hospital is today. Mickey Quinn, travelling along with a friend in a horse and carriage, saw the spectacle and told his friends, "It's Casey's new contraption. He's going to raise mashed potatoes for next season."

### Two Quinn Stories from Newspaper

The following item was published in the *Newfoundlander,* a newspaper of the 1940s and 1950s.

*This is a Mickey Quinn story. He was a famous character in St. John's many years ago, noted for his wit. Mickey, with a buddy of his, one summer in the capital, escaped the discomfort of the hot sultry nights indoors by sleeping in Buckmaster's Field, then a large expanse of grassy land in* the upper central part of St. John's but now built over. One night, Mickey retired, as usual, to his grassy bed and stretched out in a dreamless sleep. His buddy came along an hour or two later and lay down beside Mickey, who woke up just then and said, "Go back and close the gate, there's a draft in here."

Mickey Quinn did not have a permanent job, but just did odd jobs whenever he got them. He was quite big-hearted and whenever he came into a little windfall of some sort, he would always treat his friends. On one such occasion, having made a bit of money, he met three of his buddies and invited them all to come up with him to a restaurant on Water Street in the city for a scoff. The four of them went in and took a table. Mickey looked over the menu and when the waitress came to take their order, he asked, "How much are your steaks with gravy?"

She replied, "Thirty-five cents, sir."

"How much is gravy alone," asked Mickey.

"Oh, the gravy doesn't cost anything," she replied.

"Oh, if that's the case," said Mickey, "bring us four gravies."

– *Newfoundlander*, **October 1951**

## Sin!

During a Religion class at St. Pat's School, the teacher asked Mickey Quinn, "What must we do before we can expect forgiveness for our sins?"

"Sin!" replied Mickey.

## Who died?

One day in 1912 Skipper Walsh was standing outside the door of his bakery at 196 Duckworth Street watching a long funeral procession pass along the street. He asked Mickey Quinn, "Who died?" Mickey answered, "I can't say for sure, but I think it's the one in the hearse."

### Quinn for a Reference

Slacker Baird applied for a job at Goobie's Dry Goods Store on Water Street in St. John's. The manager, aware of Slacker's reputation around town, and not wanting a confrontation in the store, thought that if he demanded references, it would discourage Slacker from wanting the job. When he asked for the references, Mickey Quinn, who was standing nearby, spoke up and said, "Why, I can give Slacker a reference. His honesty has been proved over and over again. I am absolutely certain that he has been arrested eleven times for stealing and every time he was acquitted. You can't get better than that."

### Quinn at the Atlantic Hotel

Mickey Quinn sometimes slipped past the front desk at the Atlantic Hotel on Duckworth Street to find a sleeping place in a top floor storage room. John Foran, the manager, was chatting with a lady customer one morning when the sound of someone tumbling down the stairs suddenly brought the conversation to a halt. All eyes focused on Quinn as he tumbled from step to step until he landed at the bottom. Before the lady could comment, John Foran said, "Oh, that's just Mr. Quinn. He always comes down the stairs that way."

"Miss a step, did you, sir?" the lady asked Quinn.

"Not one of 'em, miss, not one! answered Quinn.

### Quinn's Medium Rare Steak

Mickey Quinn told the waiter to take his steak back to the chef because it was not cooked. A minute or so later, the waiter returned with the steak and said, "Mickey, the chef said this steak is cooked medium rare just as you ordered."

"Well, you can tell your chef that Professor Danielle had cows hurt worse than that and recovered," said Quinn.

A reading of the verses of Johnnie Burke's *Kelligrew's Soiree* will inform the reader that Burke was indeed writing about some of the characters regularly met on the streets of old St. John's. Like

Robert W. Service, Burke wasn't actually writing about these people, but used their names because they fitted his rhymes so well. But make no mistake about it; Betsy Snooks, Flipper Smith and Carolyn were as real as you and me. And they knew a good turn of phrase as well.

### Betsy Snooks

Betsy Snooks was known as the neighbourhood rat. She would gossip about everything that happened. No secret was safe with Betsy. One day she was having a cup of tea with Nancy Cronan when Nancy's husband Harry came into the kitchen. Nancy asked if she could have a bit of cheese. Harry couldn't resist it. He said, "Sure, do you want it on a biscuit or will I put it in the trap?"

### Dirty Windows

When Crooked Flavin dropped into Flipper Smith's flat at the east end of Duckworth Street, he noticed the windows badly needed cleaning. "Your window is awful dirty. You can't see out of it," he told Flipper.

"When I want to look out, I open the window," answered Flipper.

### Flipper Smith

Caroline Bouden was at wits end trying to decide on what to give her boyfriend Flipper Smith for Christmas. Her friend Kate Kelly suggested she give him a book.

"No," said Caroline, "Flipper got a book."

### Being Happy

Matty Hearn had asked Doc Neil, a character around town during the Mickey Quinn era, if his family suffered from insanity. Doc Neil answered, "Not a bit, they enjoy it."

### Little Dickie Gray

Little Dickie Gray was one of the well-known characters around St. John's in the early twentieth century. When he appeared in court, which was frequently, he always used his birth name, Richard. One such appearance in court, during the winter of 1917, is memorable more for how the newspapers reported the appearance than for the incident itself. For example, *The Evening Telegram* item appeared under the heading:

### His Request Granted

*Little Dickie Gray, a well-known character, called at the police station last night and solicited imprisonment for the winter. He is a big, burly fellow, about 35 years of age, but holds no love for work. Laziness has got the better of him and he is a worthless individual. He appeared before Charles Hutchings J.P. this morning charged with being a loose and disorderly person and was accommodated with two months.*

But was he ever rehabilitated? Some years later the following item appeared in the court news columns of *The Evening Telegram*:

*Little Dickie Gray, who by his own account has spent the greater part of the last five years as a guest of His Majesty in the Lakeside Inn, went for another prolonged sojourn to that institution today. Recently, Little Dickie went on board a schooner to meet an out-harbour friend, as he called him, and before leaving, lifted all the wearing apparel he could lay his hands on. He appeared before Judge Knight today, charged with larceny and got six months at the Penitentiary.*

Little Dickie wasn't the only one during the poverty years before Confederation who sought winter shelter by deliberately being jailed. Life behind bars with three meals a day was preferable to freezing in some dilapidated shack with insufficient food to keep body and bones together. Sometimes, entire families, after being evicted by slum landlords, would be housed in the city lock-up. And this was before the Great Depression hit.

### War Medals

Dead-eye Murphy, a war veteran, was a little peeved to see his friend, Little Dickie Gray wearing a string of war medals on his chest on Memorial Day. When he asked Little Dickie how he got the medals, Little Dickie replied, "The Government sent me this big one by mistake. The others I got because I got the big one."

### Flipper Smith

Flipper Smith took another draw on his Royal Blend cigarette and told Mickey Quinn how he expected to get Caroline Bouden to cut down on her spending. "I'll just have to put my foot down and tell her we are going to have to budget. She will just have to cut out her foolish luxuries."

A few days later Mickey asked Flipper, "Well, what was the result of your talk with the Misses? Was it effective?"

"It was. I gave up cigarettes," answered Flipper

### Little Dickie's Advice to Prison Guards

Little Dickie Gray, who was no stranger to the prison guards at Her Majesty's Penitentiary in St. John's, told a guard that the prison should ban all tin foil from coming into the prison. The most common source of supply for the tin foil was the cigarette packages that people sent to relatives doing time. The guard laughed, then picked up tin foil from a package of cigarettes and asked, "What possible harm can this do?"

"It can be used as a weapon in a prison break!" replied Little Dickie.

"Nonsense! How can a flimsy piece of tin foil be used as a weapon?" the guard asked.

"Can I show you without getting in trouble?" asked Little Dickie.

"Go right ahead. This I got to see!" said the guard.

Little Dickie quickly grabbed a sock from under his bed and hit the guard over the head, knocking him to the floor. As he helped the bewildered guard to his feet, the guard held his head and asked, "What in the name of God did you hit me with?"

"Tin foil, just tin foil. I saved up over a half pound of it and stored it in my sock. It's enough to knock any guard into a cold junk if you hit him hard enough," explained Little Dickie.

The lesson had its affect, and when the Governor of HMP learned of the experiment, he banned tin foil from coming into the prison.

### Wants a Sober Opinion

Little Dickie Gray was recovering from an operation at the old General Hospital on Forest Road in St. John's. Dr. Smith stood by his patient's bed looking very glum.

"I'm not really sure what's wrong with you, Dickie, it must be the drinking," said Dr. Smith.

"Alright, Doctor, let's get an opinion from a Doctor who is sober," commented Little Dickie.

### Slacker Baird Rescued, Then What?

It was not unusual for Slacker Baird to fall into St. John's Harbour. The following item which appeared in the *Daily News* of June 11, 1914 is a reporter's account of Slacker's brush with death in St. John's Harbour and his response to those who saved him.

### *An inebriate's narrow escape*

*Yesterday afternoon an inebriate named Baird, who divorced himself from work several years ago, fell over Crosbie's wharf and would have drowned but for the timely assistance of Mr. S. Angel and others who witnessed the happening, and went to his rescue.* Josephus *(Slacker), with two others who also believe in the maxim "Let the other fellow work and worry," was enjoying a sun-bath on the head of the pier and debating the point whether the* Karluk *made the same drift as the* Jeanette.[5] *At the same time, they were taking the soundings and temperature of a bottle of Demerara, when this youth with the historic name lost his balance, resulting in a splash and a shriek. When the inebriate came to the surface there were a few more shrieks, and in the meantime, a boat*

---

5. The *Karluk* and the *Jeanette* were two vessels lost at sea.

had been rowed to the scene, and before Josephus *sank to rise no more,* he was lifted out of the water without ceremony. When the rescuers landed him on the wharf, Baird became abusive, and Constables Stamp and Pitcher had to be called. They placed him under arrest and took him to the station where he was "hung up" to dry until this morning when he will relate his experience to Judge Knight.

For his ungrateful response to those who helped him, and his disorderly behaviour, Slacker Baird was given a week's rest at the Forest Road Hotel (Penitentiary).

### He Saw the Light

*Dead-eye* Murphy survived the Battle of the Somme. When he returned home to Newfoundland, his friends on Gower Street had a party for him. *Dead-eye* was explaining to them why he had become more religious after his wartime experiences. He said that while bullets were flying all around him, and friends were being killed or wounded, he came out of the battle without a scratch, and because of this he embraced the Lord. As the evening progressed and *Dead-eye* partook in his fair share of the *National*,[6] he became more eloquent. "See this fine tweed jacket I'm wearing, the Lord gave me this. Look at the lovely leather shoes on me feet, the Lord gave me them. Did you ever see a finer white shirt than what I got on me back here tonight? Well, I thank the Lord for giving me that. His voice grew louder and angrier as he asked, "What did the devil give me? And just what did the devil give me? Nuttin' Nuttin' at all! F- - k the devil!"

### Quinn and Sir John Crosbie

Sir John Crosbie once asked Mickey Quinn why he couldn't get a job? Quinn answered that he had tried hard to find work, but everyone wanted a reference from his last employer. "Well, can't you get one," asked Sir John?

" Impossible," quipped Mickey, "he's been dead for thirty years.

---

6. The "National" referred to rum or whiskey.

## A Guest of Sir John

It was during the Christmas Season when Mickey Quinn, while walking up Victoria Street, was invited into the home of Sir John Crosbie on that street. Sir John enjoyed Mickey's wit, and Mickey became wittier throughout the evening as he consumed drink after drink to celebrate the season. Sir John, who was on the receiving end of many of Quinn's quips, got his revenge when it came time for Mickey to leave. Being a good host, and noticing his guest had become 'tipsy,' Sir John passed him the price of a hansom (taxi) to take him to his home at Dogs Town. As Mickey left the Crosbie home, Sir John instructed him, "Now, Mickey, when you get to the corner of Prescott Street and Duckworth Street, you will see two hansoms (carriages). Take the one to the right – the one to the left doesn't exist."

## Slacker was Envious

When Slacker Baird heard of Mickey's visit with Sir John Crosbie, he was a little envious and boasted, "Sir John Crosbie spoke to me once!"

"G'wan, Slacker, what would Sir John have to say to you?" asked Quinn.

"Well, Mickey, I was down on his wharf one time, and Sir John came up to me and looked right at me and said, "Get off my wharf Slacker or I'll burst your arse'!"

## Dead-eye the Singer!

When *Dead-eye* Murphy was a student at St. Pat's School, students were asked, in turn, by a Brother to sing a song or nursery rhyme they had learned over the summer months. The session was going well until *Dead-eye*'s time came to perform. What the Brother had not known was that *Dead-eye* had lived next door to a Chinese Laundry on Gower Street and spent a lot of time at the laundry watching the laundrymen do their work. The Chinese workers entertained *Dead-eye*, who was then about nine years old, by singing nursery songs to him. By the end of the summer, *Dead-eye* knew the nursery rhyme, *Sing a Song of Six Pence* well...but in pigeon English only! He sang:

*Singee a songee sick a pence,*
*Pockee muchee lye,*
*Dozen two time blackee bird*
*Cookee in a pie.*
*When him cutee topside*
*Birdee bobbery sing,*
*Himee tinkee nicey dish*
*Setee foree King!*
*Kingee in a talkee loom*
*Countee muchee money,*
*Queeny in e kitchee,*
*Chew-chew bled n' honey*
*Servant girlee shakee*
*Hangee washee clothes,*
*Chop-chop in come blackie bird,*
*Nipee off her nose!*

### Not Alone!

When interviewing Doc Neil in his run down rented room, the welfare officer looked around at the mess, and asked, "Are you alone?"

Doc Neil, with his two hands scratching his head and under his arms, smiled and answered, "Not exactly."

### Little Dickie Gray

Little Dickie Gray walked into Truscott's Bar on Queen Street and shouted, "Anybody want a drink?"

Everyone replied, "Yes!"

"Well, go ahead," Little Dickie shouted back.

### Slacker shouts, "Help me out!"

The Statue of Industry in front of the Railway Station on Water Street in St. John's was at one time protected by a fence of vertical iron rods. Late one night, Slacker Baird, a contemporary of Mickey Quinn, had been drinking with his friends in a vacated railway car. When the time came to return home, Baird found himself holding on to one of the iron rods protecting the statue to get his balance. Then, one by one, he grabbed each rod, a process which took him around the statue more than a half dozen times. In desperation, Baird began shouting, "Help me! Help me! Somebody let me out!"

## Upstairs Light

On another occasion, Slacker Baird, intoxicated as usual, was trying to fit his key into one of the old lamp posts in the east end of St. John's. A policeman passing by decided to have some fun, and told Baird, "Well, Slacker, it seems like there's nobody home there tonight."

"Gotta be! Gotta be! There's a light on upstairs," answered Baird.

## At Casey's Saloon

Another story told about Slacker Baird involved an incident at Casey's Saloon[7] on the east end of Duckworth Street around 1906. Casey's had three entrances. When Baird arrived there intoxicated one night, the bartender tossed him out. Baird goes in a second time through another entrance and is surprised to see the same bartender who had just thrown him out. Before he could say anything, the bartender grabbed him by the collar and again tossed him into the street. Baird stands up, brushes himself off, and goes back through the third entrance. He is shocked to see the same bartender again, and as the bartender approached him, Slacker commented, "Buddy, do you own all the saloons in St. John's?"

## Slacker Baird on Doctor's Advice

Slacker Baird had gone begging to the same house several times in the same week. "Listen here," said the housewife, "why do you always come to my door to beg?"

"Doctor's orders," answered Slacker.

"Doctor's orders?" the housewife questioned.

---

7. Previously known as O'Reilley's Rum Shop on east end of Duckworth St.

"Right, ma'am. My doctor told me that when I found food that agreed with me, I should stick with it," replied Slacker.

### Robs Cop and Salvation Army!

In the court news during 1910, Slacker Baird found himself in the kind of trouble that sent him to the penitentiary. He first stole a set of salt and pepper shakers from the Salvation Army Food Depot and was arrested. Soon after, another charge was added to this when Slacker went to the home of Constable Fitzgerald in Rabbit Town and stole the officer's hay mattress. He got six months in jail for the two deeds. Slacker deliberately set out to get a jail term so he would have accommodations for the cold winter. He was not the only town character who obtained winter shelter in this way. Court records tell the story of others who did the same.

### *Dead-eye* and the Germans

When darkness fell over the battlefield during WWI, both sides would remain sheltered in the trenches and await the light of day before resuming battle. The Germans sometimes tried to anger the British forces by shouting throughout the night their slogan, "Gott Mit Uns!" which, when translated into English meant "God is with us!"

*Dead-eye* Murphy, after listening to these shouts of "Gott Mit Uns!" shouted back, "We got Mittens, too!"

### *Dead-eye* Murphy the Veteran

When *Dead-eye* returned from the battlefront at the end of WWI, his friend Mickey Quinn was there to greet him. Quinn shook his hand and said, "What a magnificent thing you've done for Newfoundland. You, me son, are one of the heroes who went over there to die for your country."

"Like hell I did, Mickey!" replied *Dead-eye*, "I went over to make some other guy die for his."

When *Dead-eye* was training with the Regiment at their camp on the banks of Quidi Vidi Lake, a strong windstorm struck the area. When the wind settled down, *Dead-eye* noticed that the lid of the soup kettle was awry, permitting dust to blow into the soup. He told the cook, "If you had put the cover more firmly on that kettle, we wouldn't get so much dust and dirt in our soup."

"Now listen to me, sonny," said the cook, "your business is to serve your country."

*Dead-eye* answered, "Yeah! But not to eat it."

### Water! Water!

*Dead-eye* Murphy was telling old war stories to his grandchildren.

"Ammunition, food and whiskey had run out and we were parched with thirst..."

"Wasn't there any water?" asked one of the children.

"Sure, but it wasn't time to be thinking of cleanliness."

### True News Item from
### *Evening Telegram*, August 21, 1912

### *Crooks Captured and Punished*

*Little Dickie Gray, aged 33; John Humby, aged 15; John Skanes, aged 18 and William Carey were before Court today and convicted of various larcenies committed. The first to stand before the bar was Humby, charged with stealing flour barrels. He was sent down for a month.*

*The next to salute His Worship was the notorious Little Dickie Gray, who broke into Ritchie's and Anderson's Offices on Thursday night, stole postage stamps and maliciously destroyed office furniture. The only evidence the police had to prove that Gray broke in was the fact that his hand was cut with glass, which was suspected to have been done while he was getting through the window. Gray denied this story. He said that he was going country-wards Thursday afternoon carrying a bottle of rum in his coat pocket when he was accosted by a bull, which gave him a* butt of his horns, broke the bottle, and in removing the debris, his hand was cut.

The Judge explained to Gray that they had much regard for him at the Pen (Penitentiary) and that if he would repeat the bull story to them, their esteem would become greater for him. The Judge gave him six months. The lad Skanes got a month in jail for theft.

The case of Carey, an old offender who was charged with stealing a coat last night, did not come off. As he was shipped to go on the Gal-a-tea *"ship in port"* today, the police authorities thought it wiser to let him go.

The police detectives deserve great credit for rounding up the culprits so promptly. William Carey had entered the hallway of a home on Princess Street in St. John's and stole a coat, which he sold for twenty cents. He used the money to buy hop beer and was drunk when the police caught up with him.

## Cuddihy says it's healthy!

Human nature is funny. When Billy Cuddihy of Flower Hill offered Tommy King a drink of wine and Tommy refused, Billy encouraged him saying, "Come on, it'll do ya good."

Tommy, who had never taken a drink before gave in. Billy offered him a second, but Tommy declined. Again Billy urged Tom, "Ah come on, have another drink — it'll do ya good." This went on for several more glasses of wine and each time Billy would pour the wine and tell Tom, "Drink it, boy, it'll do ya good." An hour later, Tom was bent over the sink and throwing his guts up and Billy was saying, "That's it, Tom, me old friend, get it all up, it'll do ya good. It"ll do ya good."

## Billy Cuddihy

Teddy Rouse and Billy Cuddihy were walking to the Liquor Store on Water Street.

"Did ya bring any money," asked Cuddihy.

"Naw, the wife blew it all on the rent," answered Rouse.

## A Great Excuse

Billy Cuddihy came home and passed his pay envelope to his wife. He was three hours late...and smelled of alcohol. When she opened the pay envelope, she counted the money and discovered that some of it had been spent. "Where's the rest of your pay?" she asked.

"Spent," said Billy.

"What did you spend it on?" she asked.

"I bought something for the house," replied Billy

"And what did you buy for the house?" she asked.

"A round of drinks," answered Billy.

## Cuddihy a Base Drummer!

During the 1920s, Billy Cuddihy played trumpet with the Catholic Cadet Corp Band. His buddy, Jack *Slinks* Murphy played the base drum. This worked out fine as long as the band played on stage, but marching on city streets presented a problem for Slinks because he was short and had trouble seeing out over the drum.

One St. Paddy's Day, the CCC Band led the St. Patrick's Day Parade on a march that went along Water Street from Patrick Street to Cochrane Street, then turned up Cochrane Street to Military Road and took a left to the Roman Catholic Cathedral. This was Slinks first outdoor parade and he had little trouble going straight down Water Street, but he encountered a problem when the parade came to the Cochrane Street and Water Street intersection. The band was playing *The Flag of Newfoundland* (Pink, White and Green) and Slinks was keeping a perfect beat with the music when the parade began turning right up Cochrane Street. All band members, that is, except Slinks. Unable to see out over the drum, he missed the turn, and continued to march east on Water Street, leaving the remainder of the band behind. When Cuddihy saw this happening, he removed the trumpet from his lips to call Murphy back, but noticed the expression of fellow band members suggesting to leave Slinks alone and let him go. Cuddihy sensed the humour in the situation and resumed playing his trumpet. When Slinks got near the Furness Withy Offices on Water Street east, a bunch of Longshoreman in the area whistled and clapped their hands for the one man band.

### Cuddihy and the Turkey

Billy Cuddihy was helping his wife Mary prepare the turkey for Christmas dinner. He was assigned the task of stuffing the turkey with dressing and then sewing it up. Billy drank a little too much of his homemade blueberry wine on Christmas Eve, and while preparing the turkey, was struggling to cope with the noisy children. "What a hangover!" Billy thought to himself. He managed to cope with it until he had completed stuffing and sewing up the turkey and attempted to get up from the table to head for the couch. However, when he stood up the turkey came with him. Billy had sewn the turkey's arse right onto his shirt. Mary managed to salvage the turkey and clean up the mess.

### Teddy Rouse

Teddy Rouse was a simple-minded character around old St. John's who made a living selling newspapers and doing errands for people. One day, while hanging around the blacksmith's on George Street, the blacksmith offered to show him how to shape a horseshoe to fit.

He told Teddy, "Now, when I take the shoe from the fire and place it on the anvil, I'll nod my head, and you hit it with this hammer." Teddy agreed.

Teddy followed the blacksmith's directions to the letter, but he never hit a blacksmith again. Neither did he ever set foot inside that Blacksmith's Store again.

### Six Months

One day, Din Ryan turned up at old Brown's Store at the Cross Roads in the west end of St. John's, after being out of the neighbourhood for a time. Old Brown greeted him with, "I haven't seen you in six months, what have you been doing?"

"Six months," Din replied.

### Quinn and Sir Robert Bond

Mickey Quinn was taking a calf, owned by Judge Prowse to its purchaser near the Market Place on Duckworth Street when he decided he wanted to obtain a quick refreshment from a nearby Inn. He stopped a gentleman and said, "Hey, mister, hold me calf for a minute, will ya?"

The Gentleman replied, "Do you know who I am?"

"Yes, I do. You are Sir Robert Bond," answered Quinn.

"Right you are. Now why did you not tip your hat," said Sir Robert.

Quinn replied curtly, " I will tip my hat, if you'll hold the calf so I can get a drink."

### A Thinking Quinn

One day Mickey Quinn was walking along Kings Bridge Road when he encountered Sir Robert Bond. Sir Robert asked, "Out of work, are you? Then you're just in time, I have a pile of wood to be cut behind my house, and I was just going to send for a man to do it."

"Is that right, Sir Robert. Where does he live? I'll go get him," said Quinn.

### Quinn and Lady Bowring

Mickey Quinn encountered Lady Bowring outside her mansion, Devon House on Forest Road and inquired about her health. "I have been very sick, in fact, I nearly died," answered Lady Bowring, "I had ptomaine-poisoning."

If she thought she had confounded Mickey Quinn, she was mistaken. Quinn came back with, " Is that so?" Then, in his most confident voice and raised eyebrows added, "What with that, ma'am, and delirium tremens,[8] a body these days don't know what he dare eat or drink."

### Professor Charles H. Danielle

Professor Charles Danielle was an eccentric of old St. John's in the late nineteenth and very early twentieth century who was well

---

8. Delirium tremens is the medical term for the DT's.

known for his humor and wit. He is best remembered in history for his Octagon Castle, adjacent to the Octagon Pond off Topsail Road, and the Royal Pavilion at Quidi Vidi Lake. He was engaged in different types of business in the city, one of these was a fruit store.

One day, a young fellow employed with a large Water Street firm was out collecting accounts and visited Danielle's Fruit Store to collect a bill from the Professor.

"The boss sent me down to get payment of his bill. He wants to close his books," said the visitor.

"Is that so?" snapped the Professor sarcastically. "He wants to close his books, does he? " Well, let him close his books. Who the blazes is stopping him? I never heard tell of closing books until I came to this country. Why, my books are open all the year round for anyone to see. Go on up and tell your boss to close his books, and when they're closed, tell him to get the biggest six-inch spike nail he can find and drive it through the cover, so they can't be opened until the Day of Judgement!"

### Rotten Apples!

A difficult-to-please, prominent lady of St. John's purchased some apples at Professor Danielle's Fruit Store. The next day, she met the Professor near the Post Office on Water Street and said, "Four of those apples you sold me yesterday were rotten. I am bringing them back."

"That's all right, madam. You needn't bring them back. Your word is just as good as the apples," shot back the Professor.

### Quinn and Professor Danielle

For a time Professor Charles Danielle operated a farm near Quidi Vidi Lake. While driving there one day in August, he met an acquaintance and invited him aboard the wagon. "I've got some men working at the hay," the Professor remarked, "and I'm taking their dinner in to them." As he had in his wagon with him two big kettles of soup, meat and potatoes, as well as another large kettle of tea and four or five loaves of bread, the acquaintance was greatly surprised upon arriving at the farm to discover only two men working there. These two men had quite a name of their own. They were the famous witty Quinns, Mickey and his brother Jack.

The Professor laid the dinner on the table, enough for five ordinary men, and then began to show his friend around the farm. They were astonished when, five or ten minutes later, there came a shot from Mickey Quinn, "Any more grub, boss?" They went into the kitchen, and there was the table cleaned off, not a morsel of food left.

"What!" exclaimed the Professor. "You've downed a sugar butt of grub already! Well, that's the limit!"

And then calling out to his boy Joe, he shouted, "For heaven's sake, Joe, go up in the loft and heave down more hay for the Quinns!"

One day while the Quinn brothers were sent to milk the cows on Professor Danielle's farm, Mickey's brother asked him how long cows should be milked.

"The same as short cows," answered Mickey.

### The Quinns at Professor Danielle's Farm

Mickey and Jack Quinn were hired to do some ploughing at Professor Danielle's farm. The two men decided that they would take turns working. Jack Quinn agreed to take the first couple of hours at the plough behind two strong horses while Mickey took a nap in the barn. Two hours later, Jack Quinn, totally exhausted, went to the barn and awoke Mickey. "How'd you get along with the work?" asked Mickey.

"I'm not getting along at all," snapped Jack, in disgust. "How do you expect me to hold a plow with two strong horses trying to pull it away from me all the time?"

### What's Time to a Pig?

One day while working on the farm of Professor Danielle, the Professor looked out through his window and saw Quinn and Joey Baird take his pigs out towards a large meadow nearby.

"Where are you taking them pigs?" asked Danielle.

"We're taking them to the meadow to graze!" shouted Quinn.

"We don't do that here," answered Danielle. "We pen them up and feed them corn."

"What for?" Quinn asked.

"It gets them fat so much faster," replied Danielle.

Not impressed by the answer, Quinn asked, "What's time to a pig?"

### Professor Danielle and Judge Prowse

Professor Danielle stopped Judge Prowse on the street and was going on and on about the problems he was having with his Royal Pavilion at Quidi Vidi Lake. Judge Prowse had listened politely, nodding at appropriate times. Sensing that the good judge was becoming a little impatient, the professor asked, "I sincerely hope that I am not unduly trespassing on your valuable time?"

"My dear Professor," answered Judge Prowse," there is a considerable difference between trespassing on time and encroaching upon eternity."

### Danielle's Bridal Suite

Professor Danielle had high hopes for the success of the bridal suite which he had lavishly furnished in his famous Octagon Castle. However, in six years the suite only brought in eight dollars and heartache for the Professor. The eight dollars came from a honeymoon couple who were charged eight dollars for two days. In addition to having the most luxurious room in the Castle, the couple were provided with room service and specially prepared meals. Upon receiving their bill, they complained it was far too expensive and suggested that one dollar per day would have been appropriate. According to the late Michael Murphy in his book *Pathways to Yesteryear*, soon after this incident, Danielle told a reporter:

This so nearly broke my heart that this suite of rooms is no longer in the market as a resort for newly wedded lovers. There will be no more "honeymoons" spent here. No, not even a *molasses moon* or a *brown sugar moon*. Henceforth, those who are reckless and foolish enough to take the matrimonial leap, must take to the woods as did our ancestors, the monkeys, for I am going to rear a couple of pigs in the bridal suite. It will pay me better.

## Reservations at Professor Danielle's

A couple from Harbour Grace spent a week at Danielle's Octagon Castle in 1900. In planning their summer stay for 1901, they wrote the Professor to make reservations. In the letter, they told how much they enjoyed their stay in 1900 and wanted to reserve the same room. However, they complained that there was a bad smell from the pig pen beneath the room's window and asked that the pigs be moved before their next visit.

Professor Danielle confirmed their reservation and added, "We have had no pigs on this property since you and your husband were here last summer."

## Danielle's Wit

Two travelers on their way to St. John's stopped at the Octagon Castle to seek a room for the night. The most abrasive of the two asked the Professor, "What does this pigsty cost for a night?"

The Professor promptly answered, "For one pig, two dollars; for two pigs, three dollars."

A lady who stopped at the Octagon Castle asked, "Can you give me a room and bath?"

"I can give you a room, madam, but you will have to take your own bath," replied the Professor.

On another occasion Professor Danielle left a note for his handyman at the Octagon Castle to carry out a described set of tasks during Danielle's absence. One item puzzled the handyman so much that he took it to a church nearby and asked the priest if he knew what it meant. The priest held the letter in his hand and read it, "The sinuosities of the aqueducts have impeded the flow of the aqueous fluid, and caused it to percolate through and injure the viaducts. Apply the appropriate remedy."

The priest explained that the recent rainfalls had caused the drains to overflow near the side of the Octagon Castle and "...blocked everything up." He told the workman that the Professor wanted the drains cleared.

The workman nodded and exclaimed, "Sure, sure, but why didn't the Professor just say so!"

### Quinn Bests Danielle

While working at the Octagon Castle, the Quinns were required to stay overnight, and the Professor provided them with a room usually reserved for staff. Next morning, at breakfast, Mickey asked the Professor, "Pardon me, sir, but with what material do you stuff the beds in this establishment?"

"Why, with the best straw to be found in all Newfoundland," answered the Professor.

"That's very interesting. I now know where the straw came from that broke the camel's back," commented Quinn.

### It's Quinn's Feather

On another occasion, the Professor told the Quinns that they would have to share a bed for the night. "Not another straw bed, I hope," said Mickey.

"No, it's an all-feather bed," said the Professor. "Have a comfortable night."

At three o'clock in the morning, Mickey awoke his brother and said, "Change places with me, it's my turn to lie on the feather."

### Cider

Mickey Quinn asked Professor Danielle, "Is there any alcohol in cider?"

"Inside whom?" replied the Professor.

### Darn the Mosquitoes

Mosquitoes were plentiful in the area of the Octagon Castle, and it wasn't surprising that sometimes they got into the food being served. A patron asked the Professor, "What are those black specks in my milk?"

He replied, "They are the vitamins that everyone has been talking about."

## When Angry

The Professor, a wordy man, struck his shins on one of the dining room chairs at his famous Octagon Castle. Noticing patrons at a nearby table, he controlled his response and commented, "Oh, the perversity of inanimate objects."

## The Professor's Wit Again!

In a letter to the *Evening Telegram*, Professor Charles Danielle admonished those patrons of his Octagon Castle who abused his hospitality. He wrote, "I want to implore patrons again not to bring flasks and bottles with them and break them around the grounds. I have buried bottles until I can't get a whole angle worm to catch a trout; they are all cut up in bits."

## Judge Prowse in Court

The following is an excerpt from a June 1893 proceeding in the court of Judge Prowse, famous Newfoundland historian. It was reported in the *Tribune*, a St. John's based newspaper.

> A small boy of 10 years had another lad of 15 up for assaulting him. The complainant could not give any account of the affair, and said he was only tickling a dog with a switch when the other attacked him.
> "Are you guilty, or not guilty?" asked the Judge.
> "He's as guilty as I am, sir," was the sturdy answer.
> He confessed to having given the younger boy a couple of "clouts," and the Judge told them both to "Get!" as the Court was not for settling disputes among boys.

## The Doctor with an LLD

Mickey Quinn, his brother Jack, and Slacker Baird were working in the field of Judge Prowse's property on Torbay Road, which is now occupied by the Salvation Army Senior Citizens' Complex. People had been coming and going all week to view the judge's oddity, a four legged duck which he had preserved in a large jar of "spirited" wine. Impressed by carriages, dress and the notoriety of the visitors, the three began to discuss the various professions of some of the visitors.

"What do the letters LLD after a person's name mean? " asked Baird.

"Dunno!" replied Jack.

Mickey, who was tossing hay into a cart while the discussion was going on, interjected, "It goes to show just how ignorant you two are. LLD means lung and liver doctor."

"Oh," responded Jack and Slacker, and the two resumed their work tossing hay.

### Quinn and Prowse

Mickey Quinn and his brother were hired to do some work around Judge Prowse's property on Torbay Road. Among the animals on the farm was a pig. The Judge assigned the Quinns a room at the rear of his residence which had its own entrance. However, Mickey became irritated when he discovered that when he left the door open to air out the room, the old pig would often wander in.

Mickey asked Prowse why the pig kept barging into the room. The Judge answered, "Well, Mickey, in the winter, that's his room."

### Go Shod the Horse

The term "shod" referred to having shoes put on a horse. One of the first assignments Mickey Quinn had when he went to work for Judge Prowse was to take the horse out and have it "shod." Later in the day, Mickey walked into Prowse's yard without the horse. Judge Prowse asked, " Quinn, where's the horse I told you to have shod?"

"Did you say shod? I thought you said shot. I've just been buryin' her," answered Quinn.

### Prowse and the Prisoner

It was often said that no other man in Newfoundland told more stories or had more stories told about him than Judge Prowse, the author of *Prowse's History of Newfoundland*.

On an occasion when he was inspecting the cells of the lock-up in St. John's, he came across a man whom he had recently arrested for his part in the famous Battle of Foxtrap. The major confrontation occurred when the railway around Conception Bay was being surveyed and the people, fearing they would lose their homes, blocked the surveying work. Judge Prowse had led a squad of police at that confrontation.

The man to whom he was now speaking in the cell was a ringleader in the affair. The man spoke up and said, "Judge, I'm all in favour of the railway now."

"Charlie, what changed your mind?" asked Prowse.

"Well," replied Charlie, "last night a drunken sailor was put in my cell. He said, "What are you in here for" and I told him for fighting the railway. And he up and told me the railway was the poor man's friend. I'm all for the railway now."

Judge Prowse, who had tried to win over the people of Foxtrap to supporting the railway, said indignantly, "Why, that's the very thing I told you!"

"Yes," admitted Charlie, "but we all knew you were paid for saying it!"

### Mrs. Brookin's Cat

Johnny Burke wrote a song called *Mrs. Brookin's Cat*. Like most of Burke's songs this one was popular in its time. The following is an excerpt from it:

*Mrs. Brookins had a pretty cat*
*She called it Tortoise Shell,*
*And it's often times I'd wish that cat*
*Was drowned in Coady's Well.*
*For 'twas at my windows early*
*I would hear her mew and chat,*
*And I only wish the devil*
*Had Mrs. Brookin's Cat.*

*With her mew, mew, in the morning,*
*And her mew, mew, every night,*
*And her clatter, clatter, clatter,*
*And her growl, growl, growl,*
*And her concert on*
*The roof till broad daylight.*

Another popular verse penned by the famous Johnny Burke was called, *Last Words of a Dying Man*. It was a short verse and reads:

*I'm dying, Kathleen, dying;*
*What was fading, now grows bright,*
*Earthly dreams on me are flying,*
*Angels I shall see tonight.*
*I'm dying, Kathleen, dying,*
*Now I hear one heavenly splash;*
*I'm dying, Kathleen, dying,*
*I'm dying my mustache.*

### Never Heard of an Elevator

An anecdote related to the elevator at the Atlantic Hotel involved the first visit of a family from Bonavista to St. John's who were among the first guests at the luxurious hotel. Azariah King, his wife and child had just arrived at the Atlantic. As Mrs. King was being introduced to the beauty salon by a hotel hostess, Azariah's attention was focused on two black doors with silver trim that would suddenly move apart and back together again by themselves. His boy asked what it was, and Azariah answered, "Well, I've never seen the like, can't say what it is!" At this point an old woman with a walking cane, glasses and grey hair stepped in front of the doors and pressed a button. The doors suddenly opened on their own, she stepped inside, and just as miraculously, the doors closed. There was a rumbling noise, and the small circled lights on top of the door began flashing. They stopped. A minute later the circles began flashing again. When they stopped this time, the door opened, and a very attractive young blond haired lady stepped out. Azariah turned to his son and said, "Quick, go get your mother!"

### Clean-Up Week with the Police

The following news item under the above heading appeared in the *Daily News* on May 1, 1914. The Clean-Up Week was not the type of event that we see being held yearly throughout Newfoundland in modern times.

*The present week is clean up week with the police and yesterday no less than six worthless vagrants, all charged with offences were remanded to the Penitentiary. Handcuffed in three pairs, four constables in charge of them, they were marched to the Penitentiary, and the sight as they passed through the streets was anything but edifying. There are a number of such vagrants still at large, and the police are engaged rounding them up.*

### Ancestry

An Englishman was having a drink at Dooley's Bar with Paddy Casey. The Englishman began to brag about his ancestry. He said, "Old chap, I'm sprung from the stock of kings. I've got royal blood in my veins. And what stock are you sprung from, Mr. Casey?"

"I'm from the Casey's," said Mickey, "and we never sprung from nobody, they sprung from us."

### Farewell to Little Dickie Gray

The last time Mickey Quinn saw his friend Little Dickie Gray, Gray was being escorted from the court room of Judge Flannery to HMP by Constable March during February 1909. Jimmy Murphy, famous song and verse writer of his time, was in court and mentioned the scene in his court news column, noting that Gray was singing as he left the court:

*Oh whiskey, you're the devil,*
*you are leading me astray,*
*Oh why to the lock up*
*You are bringing me today.*
*You've humbled me and tumbled me,*
*and robbed me of good clothes*
*Oh whiskey you have given me red blossoms on me nose.*

Gray lived on New Gower Street.

# Historical Background

### The "Real" Mickey Quinn

Mickey Quinn was a well-known character around St. John's in the early nineteenth century. He was famous for his wit and humor, and since his death on December 28, 1912, more stories have been told about Mickey Quinn than of any other character of Newfoundland history. He had a brother Jack, who was also witty, but who sometimes found himself in trouble with the police. The Quinns were famous enough to warrant special mention in local newspapers during their lifetimes. For example, when Mickey became ill and was hospitalized, the *Evening Telegram*, October 28, 1909 reported, "The well-known local comedian, Michael Quinn, who bears the stage name Dan Quinton[9], also went to the hospital today suffering from neuritis." (Inflamation of a peripheral nerve or nerves).

When Jack Quinn found himself before the courts, he, too, received special recognition in the press, as was the case in the *Telegram*, September 24, 1909, "Today before His Honour Judge Conroy, the celebrated Jack Quinn was arraigned on a charge of being a loose and disorderly person, and also for indecent exposure committed on June 19, 1909. He was sent down for six months." The term "sent down" referred to being sent to the Penitentiary. The press also referred to a person staying at the prison as being, "A guest of His Majesty." Although there are countless anecdotes of Mickey Quinn appearing before the courts, I found no records to support that he ever did. Yet, his associates were very well known in police circles, and there are numerous stories of them being "sent down" as "guests of His Majesty," in old St. John's newspapers.

Quinn performed on stage in church halls and theatres around St. John's. He appeared in Vaudeville Shows at the Nickel Theatre, the British Hall, the Casino and the Rossley Star Theatre

---

9. Mickey Quinn's obituary, December 28, 1912, *Evening Telegram* gave his stage name as Dan Quinton. However, in the *Evening Telegram* article of October 28, 1909 p4 the name is given as Dan McQuinton.

on Henry Street. In addition to performing on stage, he often worked in the ticket office at the Nickel Theatre and the Rossley Star.

Mickey Quinn grew up in the centre of St. John's at 8 Lazy Bank (Pleasant Street). He later moved to 16 Hagerty Lane which was off Pleasant Street. Both these places were located on what is now the parking lot of the Delta Hotel, just a few hundred feet from the local pub in the Delta Hotel which has immortalized his name: "Mickey Quinn's." Quinn later lived in the east-end of St. John's on two streets with colorful names, like those that might be found in a Dickens' novel. There was Brewery Lane, off "17" Plymouth Road, which today is Cook's Lane and Dog's Town, a street off "72" Plymouth Road. While living at Dog's Town, Mickey boarded with the widow Kitty Croke.

He often joked about Dog's Town on stage. He would say, "The post office had a rule that the postman couldn't knock twice on any of the doors at Dog's Town because knocking a second time could knock the house down."

Among the stories told about Mickey Quinn are those that claim he lived for a time in Boston where he married and had a son. While there is a record of a Mickey Quinn from St. John's marrying a Newfoundland girl named Shallow at Boston, Quinn's obituary stated he left no relatives other than the aunt with whom he was boarding on Queen Street.

The many stories depicting Mickey Quinn as one of the street characters who spent his day trying to satisfy his thirst for liquor do not do him justice. Quinn was not at all a heavy drinker. As Dan Quinton on stage, Mickey often portrayed an inebriate, but he was a hard-working, responsible man who sought and took work where he found it. He supported himself through odd jobs including: ticket-taker at the Nickel and Rossley Star Theatres, handyman, gardener, fisherman and seasonal cook at the lumber camp at Badger Brook.

Several of Quinn's associates often found themselves in the court reports of local newspapers in comical situations. These included: his brother Jack, Slacker Baird, Dead-eye Murphy,

Corker Tibbs, Billy Cuddihy, Teddy Rouse, Doc Neil, and Little Dickie Gray.

Mickey was well-liked in old St. John's, and some of the most prominent citizens enjoyed his company and gave him odd jobs or "hobbles" as they were called. No doubt, these associations provided so many of the Quinn stories involving people like: Judge D.W. Prowse, Professor Charles Danielle, Sir Robert Bond, Sir John Crosbie, Jack and Marie Rossley, Johnny Duff and several of the clergy. For decades after his death, newspapers carried stories showing Mickey Quinn's wit and humour.

Quinn's memory was also kept alive by a succession of after-dinner speakers up to the 1960s who kept their audiences in "stitches" with Mickey Quinn stories which they always swore were true. Many of these stories included anecdotes about Quinn during World War I and World War II, however, Quinn died on December 28, 1912 almost two years before the outbreak of war. Quinn's wit and humor were so famous during his lifetime that they inspired the stories told about him long after his death. These stories were loved and enjoyed by the public, much like the Pat, Mick and Ginger stories of Irish history, only Mickey was a genuine character with a natural talent for comedy.

Around December 20, 1912, Mickey Quinn returned to St. John's after completing a season's work as cook at the lumber camps at Badger Brook. He stayed with his aunt, a Mrs. Sam Furze, who operated a boarding house on the western side of Queen Street, which was three doors up from Water Street.

On December 28, he left his aunt's in the morning to visit the waterfront, perhaps to seek work. At around noon, he stopped to chat with a police Constable on Goodridge's Wharf, just east of Bowring's Wharf. Winds were very high that day and were getting worse as the day progressed. At 1:00 p.m., Mate Willett of the schooner *Ida B. Lynch* was putting a bowline on the vessel at the eastern most wharf when he saw the body of a man floating in the water. He immediately sought the help of Goodridge's watchman, a Mr. Parrott, in pulling the body from the water. They recognized the victim as Mickey Quinn.

Dr. O'Connell was called to the scene, and his efforts to revive Quinn were unsuccessful. Quinn's teeth had been knocked out and he had a slight cut on his head. Although the official report of Quinn's death stated he had died accidentally, for decades after, most people believed he had been the victim of a beating while visiting a ship in the harbour. The facts present a different picture.

The *Evening Telegram* December 30, 1912, reported: "The general impression amongst employees at Goodridge's premises is that the late Michael Quinn, who was drowned there Saturday, was blown over the dock in the high winds that prevailed."

In the same article, the *Evening Telegram* claimed:

It is evident that the unfortunate man struck some object when going overboard as several of his teeth were knocked out and he had a slight cut on his head. It is not unlikely that he was stunned by the blow received and thus could make no recovery.

After month's of researching Mickey Quinn's background, I still had not determined the date of Mickey Quinn's death nor had I confirmed that Mickey Quinn was a genuine wit, or the product of embellished history. Mr. L. Dohey, the archivist at the Roman Catholic Basilica, checked tombstone records of both Catholic cemeteries in St. John's, but could not find any record of Mickey Quinn. He did locate an interesting note placed in a journal at the Belvedere Orphanage by a nun. In those days, the hearse entering the Belvedere Cemetery entered through a road which passed through the Orphanage property. A nun in the convent, whether officially or not, made it a practice to enter brief details about the person being brought into the graveyard. On December 30, 1912, she noted the funeral of a Michael Quinn of St. John's, who was buried in an unmarked grave.

Armed with this date, I was able to find more details on Michael Quinn in the *Evening Telegram*. The newspaper noted, "The deceased was a local comedian, made famous in story and song and was recognized as our local comedian, being better known as "Dan Quinton" which was his stage name."

– *Evening Telegram* on December 28, 1912

This item confirmed that Mickey Quinn was a real character of old St. John's and even more, that he was, in addition to being a popular wit, a professional comedian.

It was then that I was able to end my research on St. John's beloved character, Mickey Quinn.

## The Rossley Theatres

Jack and Marie Rossley were internationally known Vaudeville Stars when in 1910 they contracted to perform at the Casino Theatre in St. John's for one month, but they were so popular that their stay was extended for nine months. In response to public demand, the Rossleys leased the Star Hall on Henry Street, added two opera boxes to the theatre and opened the Rossley Star Theatre, billed as Newfoundland's finest Vaudeville Theatre.[10] They soon added two more theatres, one at the corner of Hutching Street and Water Street called Rossley's West End Theatre, which was sometimes advertised as just "Ours" and the Rossley Wabanna Theatre on Bell Island.

All profits made during the seasons of Lent were donated to feed the poor of St. John's. In addition, they held a special night at the end of Lent when they collected bread to distribute to poor families around the city. These projects were initiated to offset some public rumblings caused by unfounded rumors that the Roman Catholic Church had condemned the Rossley Theatres.

The Rossleys were involved in raising money for multiple charitable causes, which included raising funds to send cigarettes and other supplies to Newfoundland troops overseas in WWI; raised funds for the building of a seaman's hospital and for the Church Lads' Brigade in St. John's.

The Rossley's provided good family entertainment with special matinee shows for children, and on occasions brought in circus acts, which included live animals. To help relieve the poverty situation in St. John's, the Rossleys trained and paid local children

---

10. The two opera boxes were never removed from the Star Theatre. Their history was brought to light while researching the Rossley's for this book.

to perform and involved as many as eighty of them in their Vaudeville acts.

When the Rossley's lease on the Star Hall was terminated, they rented the British Hall and opened the Rossley British Theatre. In the summer of 1917, the Rossleys closed their operations and left Newfoundland to tour Canada.

Above: A day's fishing.

Left: Transportation in the 1920s.

The first steamroller in St. John's.

*All photos courtesy of City of St. John's Archives*

Looking west on Water St. from Adelaide St.

# Chapter 2

# Wit and Humour from 1940s

The crises brought about by war carries with it a balance in the form of humour. Newfoundland in the 1940's had an influx of servicemen from Canada and the United States as well as its own soldiers, sailors and airmen. These young men and women used humour to help downplay their fears and apprehensions. The mixture of humour from far away places, with that of the battlefront humour of returning soldiers and that of our local characters, made for an interesting mix.

### Who Has Best Radio?

During the 1940s, an American soldier at Pleasantville told Ambrose, a base worker from the Southern Shore, that, "Back in the States we got radios that are so powerful you can actually hear the announcer's heart beating."

Thinking the soldier was baiting him, Ambrose said, "That's nothing, sure, up in Cappahayden, I once got Egypt on my battery radio, and in just five minutes, the sand was up to me arse!"

### Fonce Howlett

Private Fonce Howlett of Admiral's Cove and a veteran of WWII often told the story of how his unit once captured two Italian Generals.

*We were moving into a field when some Italian soldiers came out of hiding and were waving the white flag of truce. Our Captain told me to go talk with them. I approached the soldiers and asked what they wanted? The Italian officer told me they would like to change a couple of their generals for a can of condensed milk. And that's how we came to take the two enemy Generals. I'll swear on the Pink, White and Green that this really happened.*

### Poker and English Pounds

Soon after Fonce Howlett arrived in London, he found himself teaching the game of poker to a couple of British soldiers. One English soldier looked through the hand of cards dealt him and said, "I don't know your poker game, Fonce, but I'll wager a pound."

Fonce, who was holding four aces, replied, "I don't know much about your money, Mate, but I'll see your pound, and raise you a ton."

### Tea or Coffee

Fonce was enjoying refreshments at the base army canteen when he was joined by Taps Lowe, a fellow soldier from St. John's. "What are you drinking Fonce, tea or coffee?" asked Taps.

"I don't know, they didn't tell me," answered Fonce.

### Getting a Shave

Fonce was happy to return to St. John's when the war ended. One day he dropped into Harris' Barber Shop on New Gower Street. "I'll have a shave," he told Mr. Harris, as he sat himself into the barber chair.

"Didn't I shave you before?" asked Harris

"No, mate, I got that scar in France," replied Fonce.

### Who Goes There?

Fonce telling one of his war tales: "I fired a round of ten shots, then I shouted, 'Who went there?'"

### April Showers

Fonce Howlett to Doc Butler: "April showers may bring flowers, but it also wrinkles grey flannel trousers."

### Aubrey Mack

Aubrey Mack, once described as the dean of Newfoundland broadcasters, often told this story of a junior announcer who worked with him at VONF when it operated from the old Newfoundland Hotel. Mack had set up his equipment to play Vera Lynn's "White Cliffs of Dover" to be followed by a one minute silence in memory of those Newfoundlanders who had died in World War II. While the recording was playing, Mack rushed to the kitchen to get a cup of tea. He recalled, "There was really plenty of time. But all hell broke loose when the new fella went into the studio just after the minute of silence was introduced. He didn't hear the introduction, and thinking it was dead air, something totally frowned on in radio, he quickly pressed a few buttons and on came McNamara's Band."

### Swag Kenny under Attack!

Swag Kenny was a character of old St. John's who saw action overseas during WWII while serving in the British Navy. Swag was a compulsive card player and always carried a deck of cards with him, ever ready to play at anytime and anywhere. Otto Taylor, also a Navy Veteran, often told the story of a game of cards which illustrated Swag's love for the game.

Somewhere off the coast of France, Swag became involved in a poker game with his fellow seamen. In the midst of friendly chatter and the sound of a hand hitting the table as a card was laid, there was a mighty impact against the boat. All was quiet for a moment and then someone shouted, "We're torpedoed!"

All the card players, but one, jumped to their feet.

"Hold on, boys!" shouted Swag, who had remained at the table. "You can't leave me now, I've got four aces!"

### A Letter from the Battlefront

A young fellow from the Southern Shore serving with the Newfoundland Regiment in Europe during WWII sent a letter to his father:

*Dear Dad,*
  *Can you send me twenty dollars as soon as possible? I lost another leg in a gunfight with the enemy, and I am now in hospital without a penny.*
                                                          *Your Son, Charlie*

The father wrote back:

*Dear Charlie,*
  *It seems this is the fourth leg you have lost according to your letters over the past two years. You must be used to it by now. Try and get along on any legs you might have left.*
                                                          *Love, Dad*

### POW Camp Worse than Cemetery!

The following item shows how a Newfoundland boy put one over on the German censor in a prisoner of war camp. In a letter to his mother, who lived on Springdale Street in St. John's at the time, the Newfoundlander wrote:

*We are receiving the finest kind of treatment. The Germans give us the best of everything. There is only one thing that we could wish, and that is to be at Mount Carmel overlooking the beautiful Quidi Vidi Lake.*

This impressed the German censor, who sent the letter unedited to its Newfoundland address. Of course, the Newfoundlander was referring to Mount Carmel Cemetery and was communicating the message that he would rather be dead than in the German prisoner-of-war camp.

### At the Battlefront

A former Newfoundland school teacher, serving at the front during WWII, was telling his buddies how much he missed his wife. He said that she was the most perfect wife that ever lived.

"You got to be exaggerating, I love my wife too, but I can't say she is without fault. Everybody's got some fault," said his buddy.

"Well, I may have exaggerated just a little," the former teacher explained. "Absence does make the heart grow fonder, you know. If she has any little fault at all, it's her tendency to use profanity when intoxicated!"

### Famous Last Words

World War II was still fresh in the minds of Newfoundlanders in the early 1950s and wartime humour was popular. Three questions about famous wartime sayings were being asked:

(1) Who said, "We will fight them on the beaches."
(2) Who said, "I shall return."
(3) Who said, "Holy f—-k! What was that?"

**Answers:** (1) Sir Winston Churchill, (2) General Douglas MacArthur, (3) the Mayor of Hiroshima, Senkichi Awaya

### Frank Milley

Frank Milley was a well-known character in old St. John's during the 1940s. When he was first married, he was fortunate enough to rent two rooms in a furnace-heated house on Pleasant Street. After tea one evening, he told his wife, "Put on your coat, I'm going out!"

As she struggled to put on her winter coat, she asked, "Where are we going?"

Frank answered, "You're going nowhere."

"Well, why did you ask me to put on my coat?" she asked.

"I'm going out for a few drinks and I am turning off the heat," said Frank.

### Rest in Peace

Frank Milley was the fella who didn't make his wife's funeral because he was at the York Theater watching the last chapter of a Captain Marvel serial. He did, however, remember to send a wreath. He told the florist, "The ribbon must be extra wide with "Rest in Peace" on both sides and, if there is room, "We shall meet in Heaven."

The florist wrote down the message and passed it to a helper to get ready. When the wreath arrived at the Milley house where the wake was taking place, it caused quite a stir. The ribbon was extra wide as ordered, but the inscription read: "Rest in peace on both sides, and if there is room, we shall meet in Heaven."

### Forgetful

Saltwater Bill asked Frank Milley, "What's that piece of twine tied around your finger for?"

"Me wife put it there to remind me to post a letter for her," answered Milley.

"And did you mail it?" asked Saltwater Bill.

"No! She forgot to give it to me," replied Milley.

### Shoe Hospital

When a shoemaker's store named The Shoe Hospital opened in the downtown area in the early 1940s, a character called Poker Pete brought in a tattered pair of shoes to have repaired. The cobbler inspected them closely and commented, "Ya can take 'em back now, they're not worth it."

"Look ere," said Poker Pete, "the sign outside says this is a shoe hospital and I want 'em mended!"

"Oh yes," answered the cobbler, "a shoe hospital but not a mortuary."

### Seal Hunt Stowaways

Each year hundreds of sealers came to St. John's to join the sealing fleet to the annual seal hunt. These occasions were not without humour. Often the humour centered around stowaways who were usually too young to register for the hunt. One such event involved two teenagers named Dick Devereaux and Jimmy Ryall. The two went down to the wharf where the sealer *Diana* was ready to depart. There was a pile of dories and boats on the wharf ready to go aboard the vessel the next morning just before sailing time. Each dory was covered with canvas. At night, under a cover of darkness, the two boys crawled into one of the dories, pulled the canvas back over them and were prepared to stay there for the night. It was a raw and cold night, but the boys were content to suffer the hardship in order to successfully get to their first seal hunt.

At about 5:00 a.m., they heard someone shout, "OK, let's get the dories on board." Eventually their dory was lifted, moved and then clamped down hard, almost knocking their teeth out. Dick whispered to Jim, "We're aboard."

The ship's whistle blew; there was a lot of cheering, and Jimmy whispered, "She's off!"

The two remained perfectly still all day, half frozen and very hungry. They were confident that once they revealed themselves at sea, the Captain would provide them with a hot meal. At about 4:00 p.m., Dicky said, "We'd better get out now and face the Old Man. You go first, Jim."

"No, you go first," replied Jim.

"No, you go," shot back Dicky.

At this point there was the sound of a hard bump on the side of the dory. The boys looked at each other and at the same time joyously commented, "We're in the ice!" Both of them sprang out –

only to discover that they were still on the wharf, their particular dory had been left behind.

### Big Tess Face of Nineteen-Year-Old

Big Tess, a town character of the 1940s, who was often compared to Carolyn Boudin of Kelligrew's Soiree fame, lived in an attic flat near the top of Brazil Square. When she married Paddy McGrath, they slept in a hammock until they were able to save enough money to purchase a bed.

Big Tess fancied herself a raving beauty, but Paddy was always there to provide a touch of reality to Tess's fantasizing. For example, when Big Tess stopped to look into a mirror at Ayre & Sons on Water Street, she commented, "Paddy, I got the face of a nineteen-year-old girl?"

"Well, Tess, ya better give it back to her. You're getting it all wrinkled," Paddy quipped.

### Justice for Tess

On a similar occasion, after trying on the latest flower-design in a department store, she asked Paddy, "Do you think this dress does me justice?"

"It's not justice ya want Tess, it's mercy," Paddy answered.

### Paddy's Dinner

Paddy came home late for supper one night and asked Big Tess, "Is me dinner still warm?"

"It should be, I threw it in the fire two hours ago!" answered Big Tess.

### Sleeping Pills for Tess

Paddy came home with a bottle of sleeping pills which Dr. Tolson Smith had prescribed for Big Tess. Big Tess asked, "How often have I got to take these?"

"Every time you wake up," answered Paddy.

### Big Tess on the Streetcar

Big Tess was trying desperately to walk down the aisle to a seat on the streetcar, but she struggled between the narrow space between the seats. The conductor told her, "Why don't you try sideways, Tess?"

"Cause I ain't got no sideways," she replied.

She finally took a seat alongside Skinny Fagan who quipped, "They should charge by the pound to get on the street car."

"If they did, Skinny," said Tess, "you'd have to walk. They couldn't afford to stop for you."

On another occasion, a gentleman got up to give Big Tess his seat. When standing, he turned and said to her, "I beg your pardon, ma'am."

"I didn't say anything," said Big Tess.

"I'm sorry, ma'am, I thought you said 'Thank you'."

### Big Tess and the Sailor

In 1943, Big Tess, who was not yet married, was introduced to a young British sailor at a social for the troops held at the Caribou Hut, which was in the King George V Building on Water Street. Big Tess mistook the friendly nature of the sailor for a genuine interest in her. She said, "You can take me to the dance at the Star Hall tonight if you like, unless (coyly) you meet somebody more attractive in the meantime."

"I say! That's jolly sporting of you. We'll leave it like that then, shall we?" replied the sailor.

### Chicken Coup

Paddy told Big Tess that the Chicken Coup, a restaurant on New Gower Street, was serving half and half tea.

"What's half and half tea?" asked Big Tess.

"Half in the cup and half in the saucer," replied Paddy.

### Soup Time

"Paddy, didn't I tell you to let me know when the soup boiled?" Big Tess shouted.

"Indeed you did, and I'm telling you, it was at 12:30," Paddy replied.

### Big Tess at Circus

Big Tess and Paddy went to the circus that visited St. John's in 1952. Big Tess was a big woman. Regardless, she enjoyed riding on the merry-go-round, but when she got off, the horse limped. A spectator nearby commented to Paddy, "Your Misses looks a little on the heavy side."

"She's heavy on every side," chuckled Paddy. He told the man that when Big Tess was a child, her mother had to buy her back twice from the dog catcher!

### Vegetarian

Paddy told "Big Tess" that since old Rhody O'Neill had become a vegetarian, he wouldn't eat eggs because they turned into chicken. "The eggs I eat don't turn into chicken," commented "Big Tess."

"What kind are they?" asked Paddy.

"Boiled!" answered "Big Tess."

### Who's at the Door?

Paddy: Tess! There's a man at the door with a bill.

Big Tess: Don't be foolish, Paddy, it must be a duck with a hat.

### Dress to Fit

Big Tess went into the Big Six Department Store on Water Street and told the clerk, "I would like to see a dress that would fit me."

"So would I," the clerk replied.

### The Truth

Tess: "And you told me you were well off before you married me!"

Paddy: "I was!"

### Undertaker's Motto

After Jimmy Martin, the undertaker, passed away, the business was taken over by one of his employees named Billy Caul. Caul was in stiff competition with Wall's Undertaking establishment on Bambrick Street. According to the late Fred Adams, Billy Caul had a wonderful sense of humour. He adopted the following motto for his business, *Don't call Wall, phone Caul.*

## Won the Irish Sweepstakes

Bridey Murphy became rich after winning big in the Irish Sweepstakes. Her neighbours gathered at her home to offer congratulations and they wanted to know what she would do with the money. Would she buy a new house, travel, go down south to live, and would she give up her job as cleaning lady at the court house in St. John's?

"Indeed I won't give up me job, I like it too much," said Bridey, "but my attitude is certainly going to change. The Lord help that big fat-arsed judge if he happens to get in the way of me mop!"

## The Wart

A fellow was walking down Water Street with a frog sitting on his head. A man passing by asked, "Where did you get the frog?"

The frog answered, "It started as a wart on me arse!"

## The Chicken Coup

The Chicken Coup was a greasy spoon type restaurant located on New Gower Street, east of the Waldegrave Street and Daedy's Lane intersection. An American Naval officer dropped in there one evening and told the waitress, "I would like to have a nice thick, juicy steak, medium rare, with a fine lump of butter on top, and some onions."

"That would be nice, but what do you really want?" asked the waitress.

## The Effect of Alcohol

A young man from St. Anthony, with a love for alcohol, awoke one morning in a St. John's boarding house with a terrible hangover and only one dime in his pocket. He purchased a stamp and wrote his father a letter: "Dad, this time I have hit rock bottom. If

I can pull through somehow, I'll never touch hard liquor again."

Just then he spied a half-filled bottle of cheap gin sticking out from beneath his bed. He quickly downed it and sat for a few minutes pondering his good fortune. Remembering he was in the process of writing home, he added this to his letter, "And so, dad, if you need any help, anytime, just let me know!"

### Tommy Toe

Tommy Toe, whose real name was Thomas Peddle, was a renowned character of St. John's from the late 1930s to the early 1960s. He was married and had a large family. He lived on James Street in the central area of old St. John's. Tommy disappeared during the construction of St. John's Harbour. Many believed he fell asleep in an area where workmen were laying cement foundations and his presence was never noticed. Others believe he stowed away on a Portuguese boat. Although many stories are told of Tommy Toe, those whom I talked with who knew him well remembered him as an aggressive individual and say he could never match Mickey Quinn for wit and humour. Regardless, his name is immortalized as one of the interesting characters of old St. John's and the following stories, true or false, are what has kept his memory alive.

### Tommy Toe and the Cinder

Tommy Toe demanded to see the manager at the Railway Station in St. John's. He complained that he had a cinder in his eye from one of the CN engines and had to pay Dr. Tolson Smith three dollars to have it dressed. "Now, what, sir, are you going to do about it?" Tommy demanded.

The Manager replied, "Nothing, sir! Absolutely nothing! We have no more use for the cinder, and you are more than welcome to it. From a strictly legal point, the cinder was not yours, and I have no doubt that we could have you charged with removing railway property, but we will take no action against you in the matter."

### Tommy Toe at Barber Shop

Tommy Toe was in the barber's chair at Harris's Barber Shop on New Gower Street. Noticing a dog sitting nearby, he commented, "Your dog must like watching you cut hair."

Richard *Dick* Harris, the barber-owner, answered, "It's not that. Sometimes I snip off a bit of a customer's ear."

Tommy was ready for Harris at his next visit. As he was being shaved, Dick Harris asked him, "How do you find the razor?"

"Don't know I'm being shaved," replied Tommy.

"That's good to hear," said Mr. Harris.

"I thought I was being sandpapered," quipped Tommy Toe.

On another occasion, Tommy sat in the barber chair, slouched down and his eyes cast towards the floor. He had taken a few *nips* of brew before arriving at the barber shop. "I want a haircut," he said.

"In that case," said Dick Harris, "you need to sit up a bit. You're too far down in the chair for a haircut."

"Then give me a shave," muttered Tommy.

### Tommy Toe and the Pledge

During Lent one year, Tommy Toe took the pledge which meant that he took an oath never to drink liquor again. He found the temptation very strong as he neared one of his favourites, the Ritz Tavern on New Gower Street. He approached the tavern and became somewhat shaky, but after plucking up courage, he passed it. Then after going about fifty yards, he turned saying to himself, "Well done, Tom, me old trout, come back to the Ritz and I'll treat ya."

### Train for Brigus Junction

Tommy Toe boarded the Newfie Bullett in a near intoxicated state. He had been pestering the porter with a lot of questions. "Is this train going to Brigus Junction?" he asked the porter for the umpteenth time.

The porter answered, "Well, Tommy, the station-agent, the engineer, the conductor, the fireman, the waiters in the dining car and the cook all say it is going to Brigus Junction, and that's all I know."

### Tommy and the Priest

Father Power came upon Tommy Toe, who was in an intoxicated state and hanging onto a telephone pole to remain standing.

Father Power said, "Drunk again!"

"Are ye? So'm I, Father," said Tommy.

"Tch! Tch! This is not a time to be funny, Tom. You took the pledge two weeks ago that you would never take another drink. I am sorry to have to tell you this, but it's a total shame on you and a sin against God and the Church," Father Power said in a scolding manner.

"Well, Father Power," said Tommy, "are ye saying that ye are really sorry to see me in this way?"

"Yes, Tommy, indeed I am!" answered Father Power.

"Are you really very, very sorry?" asked Tommy.

"Yes, very sorry," replied the priest.

"In that case, Father Power, if you're very, very, very sorry, I'll forgive ya!" answered Tommy Toe.

### Tommy Toe and the Butt

Tommy Toe was a chain-smoker, and was known to pick up butts off the street and smoke them. He was at Ayre's Department Store one day when the Manager noticed a cigarette butt smoldering on the floor near where Tommy was standing. Pointing to the butt, he said, "Tommy, is that yours?"

"No it's not mine, sir. You saw it first. Help yourself!" answered Tommy.

### Tommy Toe before Magistrate Mulcahey

Tommy Toe was arrested for being drunk in public and taken before Magistrate Mulcahey.

"Are you positive that Tommy was drunk?" the Judge asked Constable Murphy.

"Absolutely positive," growled Constable Murphy
"Why are you so almighty certain about it?" the Judge asked.
"I saw him put a penny in the fire alarm box at the corner of Job Street and Water Street and then he looked up at the clock on the Railway Station and roared, 'Gawd, I've lost twelve pounds.'"

### Tommy Toe in Court

Tommy Toe appeared before Magistrate Billy Brown on a charge of being drunk in public.

A portion of the court manuscript read:

**Judge Brown to Police witness:** *What gave you the impression that the prisoner was worse for drink?*
**Constable Long:** *Well, your honour, he engaged in a heated argument with a taxi driver.*
**Brown:** *But, that doesn't prove anything.*
**Long:** *Well, your honour, there was no taxi driver there at all.*

Tommy was fined the customary $2.00 or a night in the lockup.

### Tommy Toe said it all!

Tommy Toe returned to St. John's after a weekend trouting on the Salmonier Line. When asked by his sidekick Fergy Murrin, "Did you fish with flies?"

"Jasus, I fished with 'em! Camped with 'em! Ate with 'em! And slept with 'em!" answered Tommy.

When Mrs. Murphy, Tommy's boarding mistress told him that she disapproved of fishing because using a hook to cut into a fish's mouth was cruel, Tommy told her, "Perhaps you're right. But if this fish had kept his mouth shut, he wouldn't be here."

### Tommy Toe and the Sweepstakes

Fifty years ago the *Irish Sweepstakes* were very popular in Newfoundland and provided very large cash prizes. Ferg Moran asked Tommy Toe what he would do if he won the *Irish Sweepstakes*.

"I'd have the park benches upholstered," Tommy replied.

### Rhody O'Neill's Bad Back

When Rhody O'Neill, alias Saltwater Bill, was asked why he didn't join up when war broke out, he answered, "I have a back impediment, sir."

"Yeah," said Fergy, "ya can't get off it!"

### Ashamed?

Judge Billy Brown: "Aren't you ashamed to be seen here in court so often?"

Tommy Toe: "Why no, your honour, I always thought it was a very respectable place."

### A Gun or an Axe?

Tommy knocked on the door of a Lemarchant Road residence and when a lady answered, asked, "Ma'am, could you be kind enough to help a poor man out of his troubles?"

"Well, I certainly would. Would you rather be shot or hit with an axe?" she answered.

### Tommy Toe Refused to Shave

A well-intentioned lady told Tommy Toe, "You would stand more chance of getting a job if you would shave and make yourself more presentable."

"You are absolutely right, madam. I found that out years ago," Tommy said.

"Really," said the lady, "have you ever been offered a job?"

"Only once, Madam. Aside from that, I've met with nothing but kindness," answered Tommy.

### Working on First Million

On another occasion, Tommy Toe was brushed aside by a well-dressed man leaving the Liquor Store at the corner of Springdale Street and Water Street.

Tommy shouted, "Look here buddy, the only difference between you and me is that you are makin' your second million, while I'm still working on my first!"

### Himself was Evidence Enough

Tommy Toe was brought before court accused of selling a bottle of rum without a license. "Look at this man," Jim Higgins, the defence lawyer argued. "Do you honestly think that if he had a bottle of rum, he'd sell it?"

The judge agreed and found Tommy "Not guilty."

### Ill Chosen Words

Dago Jones, another character from downtown St. John's, while working at the old Newfoundland Hotel, noticed a guy getting ready to jump from a window. "Can I give you a hand," he offers.

"No! I don't want a hand. I'm gonna jump."

"Can I get the police for you?"

"No. I don't want the police."

"Can I get you a priest?"

"Why would I want a priest?"

"To give you last rites."

"Last rites, what are last rites?"

"Ah, go jump ya protestant bastard! Jump!" said Dago.

### Dago had the Answer

Dago Jones was telling his buddies some of the things he had learned during history class at school. He said that the first volunteer fire department in St. John's had only a hose, a cart and four dogs. His friend *Whitey* asked, "What did the dogs do, haul the cart?"

"Nope, they searched for the hydrants," replied Dago.

### A Pig

Dago was driving along the Bay Bulls Highway when a woman driving in the opposite direction shouted from her window, "Pig."

Dago shouted back, "Slut." Then turned the next corner and ran into a pig on the road.

### A Slip of the Tongue

Paddy was sitting at bedside holding his dying wife's hand when she squeezed tightly and whispered, "Paddy, I want you to promise me one thing before I die."

"Yes, Mary, what do you want me to promise?" answered Paddy.

"Paddy, when I dies, I know you will be lonely, and, I s'pose in time, you'll find yourself another woman. If you do, I want you to promise me that you won't let her wear the clothes I'll leave behind. Now Paddy promise me that?"

"Now Mary, for Christ sake, you knows your old clothes won't fit Bessie," said Paddy.

### I'm My Own Grandpa!

Two fellows from Fortune Harbour were travelling on the Newfoundland Express. Stan says, "Well, I got it all figured out now. I married a widow, and the widow had a daughter. Then my father, a widower, married our daughter, so you understand my father is now my own son-in-law. Then again my step-daughter is my step-mother, ain't she? I am married to her mother, ain't I? So that makes me my own grandpa, doesn't it?"

"By gawd! You're right," commented his friend. And the train steamed on!

### Nora and the Ducks!

A Hamilton Cove, Notre Dame Bay lady named Nora decided to try her skills at making a homemade cake. There was a small pond on Nora's property where she bred ducks for the market. The cake came out much heavier than Nora expected. She divided the cake among several neighbours and fed the rest to her ducks. An hour later her neighbour, Katie Kelley, knocked on her door. When Nora answered, Katie said, "Nora! Nora! Your ducks just sunk!"

### Sarah and the Cow!

Sarah, a widow living at Tickle Cove, kept a cow to provide milk for her family. When the cow became sick, she sent for the

Government Veterinarian. The vet examined the cow, and gave her a bottle of medicine. He told Sarah, "The cow will have to take a tablespoon of this medicine three times a day."

"But our cow got no tablespoons. She drinks out of the bucket," commented Sarah.

On another occasion Sarah was having trouble with the chickens she kept in a shed behind the barn. She sent a letter to the Agriculture Department at the Commission of Government Offices in St. John's which read:

*Dear Sir,*
*I don't know what's happening to my chickens. Every morning when I go out back to feed 'em, I find four or five lying on the ground stiff and cold with their feet in the air. I am sending one for you to have a look at and let me know what's wrong.*
*Thank you, Sarah*

The clerk in the Government office, who received the package and Sarah's letter, after looking closely at the chicken and reading her letter, wrote back, "Dear Madam, Your chickens are dead."

An old saying at Fortune Harbour – *Love your neighbor as yourself, but don't take down the fence.*

## At the Belmont

A fella from Trepassey, a non-drinker, went into the Belmont one Saturday with several buddies who were visiting town. The guy had a very red nose, and those who knew him would never comment on it. When a longshoreman bought a round for the house, everyone took a drink except the red-nosed Trepassey man.

"Ain't you going to have a drink?" asked the longshoreman.

"I thank you, sir, but I never drink," answered the Trepassey man.

"What, you never drink?" said the longshoreman with a sarcastic laugh. "Now, if you never drink, will you tell me what makes that nose of yours so red?"

Without batting an eyelash, the Trepassey man answered, "Sir, it is glowing with pride because it is kept out of other people's business."

### Getting Up Nerve

A burly longshoreman was suffering terribly with a toothache. A co-worker urged him to go to the dentist and have it removed. "I'm terrified of dentists. I've never been to one in me life. Just the thought of it makes me nervous," explained the longshoreman.

"Look, I got a flask in me back pocket. Take a drink to steady your nerves," said the co-worker.

The Longshoreman took one drink, then another, and didn't stop until the flask was empty.

"There, my friend, how do you feel now?" asked the co-worker.

The longshoreman clenched his fist and hit it off the wall saying, "I'd like to see the son of a bitch who can take a tooth out of this head!"

### Careless Words

Judge Billy Brown pointed out that a witness was not necessarily to be regarded as untruthful because he altered a statement he had previously made. He explained, "For instance, when I entered court today, I could have sworn that I had my watch in my pocket. But then I remembered, I left it in the bathroom at home."

When he got home, his wife asked, "Why all this bother about your watch – sending four or five men for it?"

"Good heavens," said Billy, "I never sent anyone. What did you do?"

"I gave it to the first one who came. He knew just where it was," answered Mrs. Brown.

### One Skinny Pig

A man from Bay Roberts had a pig that he was fattening up to kill for Christmas. Unfortunately, in November, the man had to be taken to the General Hospital in St. John's and was not going to be released until just days before Christmas. Before leaving his home, he had instructed his two sons, "Be sure and keep the pig well fed while I'm gone. We'll be killing her for Christmas, and we want to have her good and fat." The sons vowed to do the job, and the old man went off contented to the General Hospital.

The sons did not keep their word and scarcely fed the pig. The old man returned to Bay Roberts just two days before Christmas and proceeded immediately to kill the pig. Later, he told friends, in sarcastic tones, that the pig was so thin that he had to send out to the shop and buy a couple of pounds of fatback before he could fry a piece of fresh pork.

### Swoilin (Sealing)

An American soldier, visiting a wharf at Torbay during the early days of WWII, was curious over how the men hanging out in the area supported themselves. He became involved in a conversation with one of the men and asked, "What do you do for a living here in Torbay?"

The old-timer lifted his cap, scratched his head and, after given some thought to the question, answered, "In the summer, we goes 'fishin;' in the winter, we goes 'furrin' for foxes and rabbits; and then in the spring, we goes 'swoilin'."

"Swoilin?" the tourist repeated. "How do you spell it?"

"Oh, we don't 'spell 'em'[1]," the old fisherman explained, "we hauls 'em."

### The WDITTY!

Just before Confederation, a fellow from Joe Batt's Arm in Fogo District went out on the squid jigging grounds in a brand new punt. In a boat near him, when he drew up on the grounds, there

---

1. The term 'spell 'em' meant to carry something.

was a fisherman who began to admire the new punt, and who noticed on the bow of the boat, the letters "WDITTY."

He was curious by the unusual word, and supposing the letters spelled the boat's name, and not being able to make out what word they spelled, he shouted to the boy and asked him what they stood for.

"What Difference Is That To You," the boy answered.

"I'll tell you, little spalpeen, what difference it is to me if I get hold of you!" roared the angry fisherman as he rowed towards the punt.

The young fellow was able to reason with the fisherman and persuaded him that the letters stood for the name of the boat, which was "What Difference Is That To You." The explanation was just in time because in another minute, the fishermen had planned to teach him a lesson he wouldn't forget.

In a similar case, a man at King's Cove owned a dog. Whenever anybody would inquire what the dog's name was, the owner would answer, "Ask-em." The answer raised eyebrows and angered some, but they soon learned that "Ask-em" was the dog's name.

### Washington a General or Admiral

A Bonavista school teacher, while teaching a history lesson, asked the class if anyone could tell her whether or not George Washington was a great General or a great Admiral?

The son of a prominent fishing captain in the community raised his hand and the teacher told him to stand up and answer the question. The boy stood up and said, "George Washington was a great General, ma'am. I saw a picture of him crossing the Delaware, and no great Admiral would put out from shore standing up in a skiff."

### Island Cove Wit

The following two stories illustrate the wit of the people of Lower Island Cove. The first is as follows:

A Lower Island Cove man, known for his cleverness in mathematics, went into the woods with his horse and slide to gather wood. A neighbour's young son tagged along to help. Suddenly, the boy said, "Look, Mr. Hatch, your horse is lame."

"Not at all," said Hatch, "he's doing a sum."

"Doing a sum?" says the boy. "How do you figure that out?"

"Can't you see, he's putting down three, and carrying one," answered Hatch.

The second story is about a Lower Island Cove man who left Newfoundland for the Boston States.[2] After arriving in the city of Boston, he went into a wholesale establishment by mistake to buy something, and after a considerable amount of time looking around, he had not seen one retail article for immediate sale. He turned to the three clerks who were there at the time and exclaimed in a surprised tone, "What do you fellas sell here?"

Now the clerks figured him for a *bumpkin* and one winked at the other two, as much as to say, let's get a rise out of this green newcomer. So he spoke up and answered, "Monkey."

The Newfoundlander sized up the situation for a few moments and then casually said, "Well fellas, it's wonderful to see you're doing such a good business, there's only three of you left," and he walked out.

A Lower Island Cove man was in court accused of stealing a neighbour's chicken. He was defending himself. After listening to his accuser in the witness stand, he asked a few questions.

"Did you see me go into the hen house?" he asked.

"Yes, I did!" the witness answered.

"Well...did you see me come out?" asked the accused.

"Why no, I didn't," answered the witness.

"Your honour, that's my defence. I'm still in the henhouse," concluded the accused.

---

2. Pre-Confederation Newfoundlanders referred to Boston as "the Boston States."

A fella from Lower Island Cove went into a St. John's department store and asked for some pillow slips. The clerk asked him what size he needed. The man replied, "I'm not sure, but me wife wears a size seven hat."

When the man returned home, he found his wife sitting at the kitchen table weeping, "My gawd, George, the cat ate your dinner," she said.

"Ah, never mind Mary, we can get a new cat tomorrow," said George.

A tourist visiting Lower Island Cove, after looking around the area, asked George, a local fisherman, "Whatever possessed you to be born in a place like this?"

"I wanted to be close to me mother!" answered George.

### Lost and Found

A fellow from Bonavista approached a clerk at the Railway Station in St. John's and said, "I left a bottle of Screech in the train when I arrived here this morning. Was it turned into the lost and found department?"

"No," answered the clerk, "but the fellow who found it was."

### When Medical Service Given by Mail

Tom Chafe was employed as a fire-warden in Central Newfoundland during the 1920s. When he developed some bad back pains, he sent a letter of request to the General Hospital in St. John's looking for a plaster, which he believed would ease his pain. Chafe, however, could neither read nor write, so he got a fellow worker to pen the letter. Just a few days after the letter was mailed to St. John's, he received a poster in the mail from the Department of Natural Resources in St. John's with the words "Prevent Forest Fires" in large black type on it.

Unable to read the poster and thinking it was the plaster for his back, Chafe promptly got some flour paste and plastered it on his back. As he did this, he wondered why there wasn't some glue or something on it to make it stick. A day or two later, the real plaster arrived and he stuck it upon a tree, thinking it was the fire prevention poster he usually received that time of year. He was curious as to why the department had been so thoughtful as to provide glue on the back of the poster to make it easier to stick on a tree or post.

When his back got worse, he went to the Doctor at Grand Falls. He explained about the plaster, and so on. The expression on the Doctor's face suddenly changed. It was as though he was holding his breath. The Doctor tried to contain his laughter, but he couldn't, and suddenly roared uncontrollably. The incident inspired Chafe to learn to read.

### The All-Penny Jury

This story was told for decades when the Supreme Court on Circuit used to travel around Newfoundland annually. They found themselves in Carbonear one year where the Penny name was the most common name in the area. The Court was selecting a jury for a scheduled trial. The Judge sang out, "Call the jury."

"Gentlemen," instructed the clerk of the Court, "answer to your names.

First, James Penny."
"Here, sir."
"Alfred Penny."
"Here, sir."
"Richard Penny."
"Here, sir."
"John Penny."
"Here, sir."
"William Penny."
"Here, sir."
"Abraham Penny."
"Here, sir."
"Joseph Penny."
"Here, sir."
"Robert Penny."

"Here, sir."
"Joshua Penny."
"Here, sir."
"John Penny of William."
"Here, sir."
"John Penny of John."
"Here, sir."

When the roll call was completed, the clerk reported, "My Lord, the panel is exhausted and we need one more juror."

"Then close the doors and call someone within the hearing of the Court to complete the Jury," ordered the judge.

The under-sheriff thereupon brought one of the spectators to the front, and the Clerk asked, "What is your name, sir?"

The man truthfully replied, "Alfred Halfpenny."

At that time, there were only a few families of Halfpenny in Carbonear, and since that time the name has died out.

## News Bulletin

A radio news bulletin reported that two men had escaped from Her Majesty's Penitentiary on Forest Road. One prisoner was six feet tall, the other four feet. Aubrey McDonald reported, "The police are looking high and low for the escaped prisoners."

## Ingenuity

The landlady at a boarding house in St. John's was having difficulty finding a tactful way to tell her new boarder that he smelled and should wash. Tommy, her husband, offered to handle the problem.

He asked the boarder, "What is frozen tea?"
"Iced tea," the boarder answered.
"What is frozen beer?" asked Tommy.
"Iced beer," answered the boarder.
"What is frozen ink?" asked Tommy.
"Iced ink," the boarder replied.
"Dat you do, a good wash will cure the problem!" said Tommy.

## The Old Fire Place

Many houses in pre-confederation Newfoundland relied on open fireplaces during the winter. The following verse about Willie and a fireplace was popular in the 1930s.

*Little Willie, in bows and sashes,*
*Fell in the fire and got burned to ashes.*
*In the winter, when the weather is chilly,*
*No one likes to poke up Willie.*

## After the Angelus, Please!

Two long time friends and neighbours who lived in Bay Bulls were divided over the referendum issue of 1948. Mazie was strongly against joining Canada while her neighbours were just as strongly in favour of Confederation. The dispute caused the breakup of a life-long friendship and the start of a bitter relationship. The neighbour had left a rather large fishing boat on a piece of property, half of which Mazie claimed she owned. Despite her best efforts to persuade the neighbour to remove the boat, he flatly refused.

Mazie decided that if the neighbour was not going to move the boat off her half of the property, she would take matters into her own hands. One day she turned up at the boat with a saw and began sawing it in half. At 12 noon, the Bay Bulls Roman Catholic Church began tolling the bells to announce to the Catholic community that it was time to say the "Angelus."

Mazie, a devout Catholic, dropped her saw, and knelt down to pray.

When she was finished, she blessed herself, picked up her saw and completed sawing the boat in half.

## At The Brownsdale Hotel

Two sealers, George and Bill, from Conception Bay North came to St. John's in the 1940s to register for the annual seal hunt. They were a day early and, not knowing anyone in St. John's had to find a hotel for the night. They turned up at the Brownsdale Hotel on the corner of New Gower Street and Brazil Square. The two had been drinking at the Green Lantern Tavern, near the War Memorial on Duckworth Street and were struggling to be coherent.

George told the clerk, "Just a minute. What we wansh ish a bed with two rooms."

"I think what you want is a room with two beds," the clerk said.

George and Bill nodded their approval, and a few minutes later, fully dressed, they were stretched out in the same bed.

"Shay, George, there's somebody in my bed," said Bill.

"Shinsh you mentioned it, old man, ther'sh somebody sleeping in mine too," responded George.

"What'sh you say, let's kick 'em out," said Bill.

There were sounds of a terrific struggle.

"Shay, Bill, I got mine out!" George said.

"Good show, old man. But I can't handle mine, he pushed me out," answered Bill.

"That's all right, pal, I got rid of mine, you just come and sleep with me," offered George.

### Unusual berth

A man had just purchased the last sleeping car space on the Newfie Bullet or Newfoundland Express. The next customer, an old lady, begged him to sell her the ticket. She said that because of her poor health she had to have a berth on the train. Being a true gentleman, the man agreed and sold her his ticket. He then went to the station office and phoned into VOCM requesting that a special message to his wife be included in their evening broadcast, which always featured a segment for such messages with the requirement that they be as short as possible.

The message that went out over the air waves that night read: "To Mary in Gambo, 'Will not arrive until Wednesday. Just gave berth to an old lady.'"

### Letter from Mom

A young man from Grand Falls, working in St. John's, received a letter from his mother which read:

*Dear Michael,*
   *A lot has happened since you left home. Your father got a new job. I got all my teeth out and a new oil stove put in ..."*

## A Remedy – Perhaps?

During WWII, a member of the Quebec Legislature suggested that since Canada was helping to defend Newfoundland, Labrador should be given to Quebec. That idea drew criticism in Newfoundland and the following letter appeared in the *Daily News* in March 1943.

*Dear Sir:*
   *One should be amused, mingled with a bit of surprise, to read in a late newspaper dispatch that an honourable member of either the Quebec or Ottawa House of Parliament said, "Newfoundland should give Labrador to Canada in return for the protection that Canada is giving Newfoundland," or something to that effect. The incidents of the little blowing up of ships on our coast, including the* Caribou, *are shining examples. Why then should we not have a little "swop" all around? Give the United States, Nova Scotia and Prince Edward Island in exchange for the protection the United States is giving. Dear me! Has our present system of government gotten so decrepit or so poor "as none so poor as to do us reverence." I think the honorable and wise gentleman should try "Brick's Tasteless," they say it makes the weak strong and is good for anemia and particularly good for flatulence.*
                              *Yours truly, F. F. Jardine*

## St. John's Man Defends Hollywood Star

When Joan Blondell, one of Hollywood's top stars of the 1940s visited American troops in Newfoundland during WWII, she picked up an often-used local phrase, "Stay where you're to, and I'll come where you're at," while entertaining the soldiers. Most Newfoundlanders enjoyed the humour, but some were upset.

During February 1942, Miss Blondell hosted "Command Performance," a radio show broadcast across the United States, Canada and Newfoundland, and she sang, "The Newfoundland Express" which described the Newfoundland train as the *Newphie Bullet* (sic). She also poked fun at New York, Texas and Brooklyn. Apparently, this was too much for some Newfoundlanders, who sent off anonymous letters cursing the star.[3] Other Newfoundlanders came to the movie-star's defence.

George Ayre of St. John's penned an eloquent letter defending Blondell, which was published in the *Evening Telegram* in March 1943. In part, it read, "It is a great pity that our cowardly, anonymous writers did not bless instead of curse, but that they did not. I am prepared to do it for them, and in my simple humble way say:

> "May heaven bless you Joan Blondell,
> Your form and acting are both swell,
> Let those who curse you go to
> Joe Batt's Arm,
> And there I bet, they'll do no harm,
> Come back and with us long do well
> For we all love you Joan Blondell."

### The Bastard

Sir Gordon MacDonald was not a well-liked Governor of Newfoundland. In addition to raising the ire of anti-confederates, many viewed him as being arrogant and disrespectful of Newfoundlanders. Once, while speaking at a church gathering, he referred to "...the wine bibbers of the East End and the beer guzzlers of the West End." He forbade the use of alcoholic beverages at Government House receptions. When he departed from Newfoundland at the end of the Commission of Government era, the following acrostic slipped by editors at the *Evening Telegram* and was published on May 8, 1949.

---

3. The story of Joan Blondell and the Newfoundand Express is told in *Newfoundland Adventure Stories, In Air, On Land, At Sea* by Jack Fitzgerald.

*The prayers of countless thousands sent*
*Heavenwards to speed thy safe return,*
*Ennobled as thou art with duty well performed.*
*Bringing peace, security and joy.*
*Among the peoples of this New Found Land,*
*So saddened and depressed until your presence*
*Taught us discern and help decide what's best for*
*All on whom fortune had not smiled.*
*Remember, if you will, the kindness and the love,*
*Devotion and the respect that we the people have for thee.*
*Farewell!*
– Beyond Belief, Incredible Stories of Old St. John's
by Jack Fitzgerald

### Good Guess!

Everyday, like clockwork, Skipper Murphy made his way down to Steer's Wharf in St. John's Harbour at 1:00 p.m. where he would spend a few hours chatting with old timers and fishermen. At 4:00 p.m., he began his walk up the hills to his home off Brazil Street in time for supper. One day, while walking up Caul's Lane, off Central Street, he ran into three neighborhood teens: Stan Dooley, Whitey Reardigan and Jimmy Lundrigan. The young trio always enjoyed conversation with the Skipper. During their chat on this day, Whitey said, "Skipper, I bet you fifty cents that not only can I tell you how old you are, but I can tell you on what date your birthday falls?

"You got a bet, young fella!" said Skipper.

"First, Skipper, let me see your tongue? Asked Whitey. Skipper stuck his tongue out and Whitey inspected it and said, "Hmmmm! Now turn around and drop your pants down." Skipper did as he was requested.

"Good enough, I got it all figured out now. You are seventy-four years old and your birthday is on October 14," concluded Whitey

"Amazing, absolutely amazing!" said Skipper as he passed

Whitey a fifty cent piece. "But how in the name of the Lord were you so accurate?"

"Simple! You told me yesterday!" Whitey said as he pocketed his winnings.

### Cat Kills Dog

Angus pounded on the door of a dog owner. When the man answered, Angus gulped as he came face to face with a huge, muscular, and aggressive man. "Do you own a Doberman Pincher?" Angus meekly asked.

"Yep, what's it to ya?"

"Well, my cat just killed it."

"Idiot! How can a cat kill a Doberman?"

"It got stuck in his throat!"

### Shoes?

Harry: "George, I remember when your Aunt Kitty sent you your first pair of shoes, and your mother sent them back because there was no instructions with them!"

George: "Yes, Harry, and when she sent them back and I put them on, you asked me what they were?"

### Fifty Cents is Not Much

*I took Daisy Caul to the B.I.S. Hall*
*It was a social hop.*
*We waited till the folks got out,*
*And the music it did stop.*
*Then to the Stirling we went,*
*The best restaurant on Water Street.*
*She said she wasn't hungry,*
*But this is what she eat:*
*A dozen raw, a plate of slaw,*
*A chicken and a roast,*
*Some apple sauce and Asparagus*
*And fresh sardines on toast,*
*A pot of stew, and crackers too,*

*Her appetite was immense!*
*When she called for pie,*
*I thought I'd die,*
*'Cause I had but fifty cents.*

*She said, "Oh I'm not hungry!"*
*And she didn't care to eat,*
*But I've got money in my clothes*
*To bet she can't be beat.*
*She took it in so cozy,*
*She had an awful tank,*
*She said she wasn't thirsty,*
*But this is what she drank:*
*A whisky skin, a glass of gin,*
*Which made me shake with fear,*
*A ginger pop, with rum on top,*
*A schooner then of beer,*
*Then six Haig Ale, a gin cocktail;*
*She should have had more sense,*
*When she called for more,*
*I fell on the floor,*
*Cause I had but fifty cents.*

*Of course I wasn't hungry,*
*And didn't care to eat,*
*Expecting every moment*
*To be kicked into the street.*
*She said she'd fetch her family round,*
*And some night we'd have fun,*
*When I gave the man the fifty cents,*
*This is what he done:*
*He tore my clothes,*
*He smashed my nose,*
*He hit me on the jaw,*
*He gave me a prize*
*Of two black eyes*

*And with me swept the floor.*
*He took me where my pants hung loose,*
*And threw me over the fence,*
*Take my advice, don't try it twice*
*If you've got but fifty cents.*

– Anonymous

### Not Musically Inclined

Frank Murphy was visiting friends on Craigmillar Avenue. The lady of the house, who was proud of her piano playing ability, had just finished a medley of Chopin, Beethoven and Strauss. She turned to Frank and asked, "Would you like a sonata before we serve dinner?"

"I had a couple on my way here, but I think I could stand another one!" replied Frank.

### The Englishman at the Cochrane Hotel

An Englishman staying at the Cochrane Hotel in St. John's during the 1940s became friendly with the clerk at the hotel and the two often entertained each other with jokes and riddles. One day the clerk called the Englishman over and said, "Here's a good riddle for you. My mother and father had a child, but it wasn't my brother and it wasn't my sister. Who was it?"

"I don't know. Who was it?" asked the Englishman.

"It was me."

The Englishman was much amused and upon returning to England tried the joke out on one of his friends.

"Look here," he said, "I heard a jolly good riddle in Newfoundland. I'll spring it on you. My mother and father had a child and it wasn't my brother and it wasn't my sister. Who was it? Give up? Give up."

"Yes, I give up," said the friend.

"Ha! Ha! It was the clerk at the Cochrane Hotel in St. John's," said the Englishman.

## No Whiskey Today

Tommy Toe found himself on Bowring's Wharf alone and with a bottle of whiskey. He considered himself blessed! He had just taken his first mouthful when an out-harbour man came along and sat down beside him, "What are ya drinkin' there, fella?" he asked.

"Whiskey," answered Tommy.

"Ya know, I'm seventy-two years old and never tasted a drop of whiskey," commented the visitor.

"Dat so!" said Tommy. "Well don't worry yourself, cause you're not going to start now."

## WWII Joke

Tom and Mary were two Newfoundlanders stranded in Berlin when WWII broke out. Tom was walking along a side street in Berlin one day and was astounded to come face to face with Adolph Hitler. When Tom failed to address Hitler with the appropriate salute, Hitler drew his gun and asked, "Where are you from?"

"I'm from Newfoundland, sir," answered the frightened Newfoundlander.

"Are you from German stock?" asked Hitler.

"No, sir. I am of English descent," answered Tom.

"English! An Englishman!" shouted Hitler. He pointed his gun at Tom's head and walked him to a nearby field, where there was a ton or more of horse manure piled high, and ordered Tom to eat every bit of it. Tom reluctantly got on his hands and knees and began eating the manure. Hitler laughed so heartily that he dropped his gun. Tom seized the moment and grabbed the gun and turned the tables on Hitler. "It's your turn to eat," said Tom as he pointed the gun at Hitler's head.

Hitler fell to his knees and began eating. Tom quietly laid the gun on the ground and turned and ran from the scene. He ran down a long street, cut into lane ways and jumped over fences and went up the rear fire escape of the hotel where he and Mary were staying. "Mary! Mary!" he said excitedly, "you'll never guess who I just had lunch with."

## No Fear of Dentists

Frank Milley rushed into the office of Doctor Darcy, a dentist, and said, "Doc, I got to have a tooth pulled right away, we've got to catch the train. Just pull it out quickly and don't bother with an anesthetic. We haven't got time."

"That will be very painful without an anesthetic," said Dr. Darcy.

"Don't worry about the pain, just get it out as fast as you can," said Frank.

"You are a very brave man, Frank. Now, tell me which tooth you want out?" asked Dr. Darcy.

"Mary, get in the chair and show Dr. Darcy your bad tooth," said Frank.

## Victor Mature

Victor Mature was one of Hollywood's top stars for several decades. In 1943 he was stationed at Argentia. He worked on a boat numbered "103" which carried munitions to American batteries around Newfoundland. Frequently, his boat would tie up at the Army Dock in St. John's and the movie star availed of the opportunity to visit the city. Mike Cahill and Joe O'Toole worked at the Army Docks at the time and got to know Mature during his visits. They both recalled him as being an ordinary type guy with a great sense of humor. The two men recalled one encounter with the star when he was trying to line up a date for the evening. At the time, Victor Mature's fame had reached Newfoundland and his movies were playing in St. John's theatres. Cahill recalled that Mature had an address book with a list of girls names from which he tried to arrange a date. After just a few calls, the Hollywood star was in fits of laughter. He told Cahill and O'Toole that the girls he had called did not believe they were actually talking with Victor Mature.

He called a girl named Marie and said, "Marie, this is Victor Mature, a friend gave me your number and I would be very happy if you would join me for dinner this evening at the Newfoundland Hotel?"

"Who did you say you were?" asked Marie.

"Victor Mature."

"So's your father!" Marie answered and hung up the phone.

He then called a girl named Betty. "Hello Betty, a mutual friend gave me your number and said I could call and invite you out to dinner."

"Who is this?" Betty asked.

"Victor Mature," replied the movie star.

"Victor Mature the movie star," said Betty

"Yes, that's right," said Mature.

"Oh I'm sorry I can't dine with you tonight, I'm having dinner with the King of England," said Betty as she slapped down the receiver.

He then called a girl named Helen and once again asked, "Hello Helen, this is Victor Mature, a mutual friend gave me your number and I would be honoured if you would join me for an evening on the town."

"Are you a Yank," asked Helen.

"Yes, I am," answered Mature.

Before he could say any more Helen asked, "What time can you pick me up?"

This time Mature, in fits of laughter, hung up. Mr. Cahill said that Mature thought the reactions were hilarious. He did find a girl who took him seriously and after a rather long conversation on the phone agreed to go to dinner with him.

Mature and his date ended up dining and dancing at the Newfoundland Hotel. At the end of the evening, the girl asked him, "Would you like to come up to my house?"

"Well, what's in it for me?" asked the Hollywood star.

"There's not much in the house, but I suppose I could give you a few lemon cream biscuits," replied the girl.

Victor Mature became friends with radio announcer Aubrey McDonald. In 1943 the Newfoundland Broadcasting station was on the top floor of the Newfoundland Hotel. Mature arrived at the Hotel one Friday evening and after booking a room called his friend, who had agreed to take him to some of the City's finest night spots. McDonald got off work and went to Mature's room. Mature went down to the Hotel Bar while McDonald took a bath. A hotel employee noticed that the room door was opened and went inside. He asked McDonald what he was doing in this room taking a bath. McDonald answered, "I'm a guest of the Hollywood movie star, Victor Mature." The employee was not yet aware that the star was in Newfoundland and replied, "You're a God damned fool, get yourself dressed and get out of the room!"

As the employee was leaving, Victor Mature was entering. The employee asked, "And who are you?"

"I'm Victor Mature," said the man.

"Well, you're a bigger fool than he is," the employee said as he left the room in disgust.

## Ned Converted

Ned worked as a longshoreman on the St. John's Waterfront and was known for his bad language. He would punctuate all his comments with 'f___k' this, or 'f___k' that, every sentence uttered included the word 'f___k.' When the Salvation Army band began visiting the waterfront, Ned began to listen and was so impressed that he converted and took up playing the base drum in the band. On an occasion when the band stopped at Steers' cove and attracted a big crowd, Ned was called upon to tell how he became a convert. He went on and on about how sinful he was and in particular he talked about his use of bad language. Then his pride and excitement grew as he told how he joined the Salvation Army after seeing the light. His voice reached a high pitch when he said, "I am overjoyed. I am so filled with the joys of Jesus I could just put my foot through this 'f___in' drum."

## Busy Wife

Jimmy, a longshoreman, came home from a hard day's work and said to his wife Mary, "I'm sick and tired of you bending over that hot stove all day long. Straighten up, girl!"

## Parish Dues

The parish priest at Cappahayden had a novel approach to collecting his annual dues from parishioners. He kept two separate listings of people. One listed the most devout members of his parish, and the second listed those of moderate faith. The first list he filed under the heading, "Top Sacred" and the second listing was filed under the heading, "Sacred."

## School Song

Several St. Patrick's Convent students found a way to raise money for a May 24 camping trip. One of the girls had found a bottle of whiskey hidden near a tree on Monk's Lane. The girls decided to raffle it off among the students at Holy Cross School, which was located across the street from their school.

One of the students at St. Patrick's saw humour in the situation and penned what she called the convent's school song:

*We are brave, we are bold,*
*When there's whiskey to be sold*
*in the cellars of St. Patrick's School.*
*Run, Run, Run,*
*I think I hear a nun,*
*Pick up your whiskey and run.*
*If Father Bradshaw should appear,*
*Tell him its just Spruce Beer*
*In the cellars of St. Patrick's School.*
*Rah! Rah! Rah!*

## Brewis

Brewis was always a popular Newfoundland dish, even during hard times. The following tribute to this dish appeared in the *Evening Telegram* in 1948 under the pseudonym Nemo Dixit:

*Let the Scotchman have his haddock,*
*yea his shortcake and his haggis*
*And the Irish keep their bacon,*

*their pitaties and their stews.*
*While the Briton has permission to*
*eat his beef and pickles,*
*For these are not my fancy,*
*give me a plate of brewis.*

*When Robbie praised the haggis,*
*the blythe and bonnie haggis,*
*And Shakespeare painted Bacon*
*in his very richest hues,*
*When Lamb was fond of cutlets,*
*or if not it doesn't matter*
*They did these things 'cos none*
*of them had ever eaten brewis.*

*When the snows of cruel winter,*
*drifts in hillocks round the window*
*And the wind is shrieking madly,*
*fairly yelling down the flues,*
*Then strangers 'gin to shiver, but*
*not so the Newfoundlander.*
*'Tis his music and his paintings,*
*and he likes it with his brewis.*

## A Lot of Crap

'Twas the night before Christmas and all through the house, not a creature was stirring not even a mouse. At 2:00 a.m. Christmas morning, if the occupants of number one Damerill's Lane in downtown St. John's were expecting the sound of sleigh bells on their roof, they were not entirely disappointed. At 2:00 a.m. sleigh bells were heard, followed by a crashing sound and the pounding of Reindeer hoofs? Well, not really Reindeer hoofs.

What interrupted the solitude of Christmas night was a horse and wagon crashing through a front room window. The impact shook the entire house and caused the ceiling in the room to collapse. Dishes on the sideboard in the kitchen fell to the floor and smashed. Just as suddenly as it happened everyone in the house was awakened, but there were no gifts in the wagon of this sleigh. It was one of the City of St. John's famous *honey wagons,* which collected night soil from homes without sewerage. Its contents spread everywhere, along the street outside there was a trail leading to the house, and the remainder of the contents ended up inside the house.

According to the *Evening Telegram* of December 28, 1940, the sleigh was doing its rounds on Wickford Street and while crossing Lime Street, slipped on ice and ended up going out of control into number one Damerill's Lane. Neighbours came to the aid of the family to make sure they had a Merry Christmas.

### Strong Anti-Confederate

St. John's was a stronghold for the anti-confederate movement during the battle leading up to the Referendum of 1948. An example of just how deep the bitter feelings went can be found in following anecdote about a case before Magistrate's Court.

The victim of rape was describing to the court the circumstances under which the crime had taken place. She was working in a fourth floor office of a building on Water Street when Joey Smallwood was leading a parade of pro-confederates up Water Street. Smallwood was speaking over a public address system from the back of a truck which was decorated with Confederation posters. The witness said she bent over to look out the window to see the parade below, when the office boy came up behind her, shut the window down on top of her head and proceeded to commit rape. The judge asked, "Did you put up any kind of a struggle?"

"I tried, but the window was holding me down," the witness answered.

"Well, did you not shout out for help, there was a parade and hundreds of people on the streets?" asked the judge.

"What? Me shout out and have that bastard Smallwood think I was cheering for him!" the witness responded.

A streetcar in St. John's.

The Newfie Bullet.

*All photos courtesy of City of St. John's Archives*

Above: Style of dress for the period.

Below: Central Fire Hall, St. John's.

# Chapter 3

# Wit and Humour from the 1950s and 1960s

The neighbourhood boundaries of old St. John's changed rapidly after confederation due to the expansion and growth of the city. In the 1950's and 1960's, the centre-town boundaries were Springdale Street on the west, Carter's Hill on the east, LeMarchant Road on the north and the Waterfront on the south. It was in this area where I grew up and where some of the stories in this chapter originated. Because of my familiarity with the old part of St. John's, I remember well the names of the people there and the stories of wit and humour associated with each one and which were so popular in that era. These stories, like the many others in this chapter, form a wonderful part of our Legacy of Laughter.

## Fatso and Murphy

Fatso Ryan was not a good card player but that wasn't reason enough in a card game one evening for his partner, Jack Murphy to read the Riot Act to him every time Fatso made a mistake. After a particularly bad play, Murphy turned upon Fatso with gnashing teeth and said, "Fatso, why in the name of Jasus didn't you follow my lead?"

Fatso, still a bit confused and peevish about Murphy's harassment, replied, "If I follow anybody's lead, believe me, I'll be anybody's but yours."

Murphy snorted and subsided. But, in the next hand, after an inexcusable faux pas, he threw down his cards in desperation. "For the love of Christ, Fatso," Murphy cried, "didn't you see me call for a spade or a club? Haven't you any black suit at all?"

"Sure," came back Fatso, with a delightfully annoying yawn, "but I'm keeping it for your funeral."

## Explaining Miracles

During Religion class at the old Holy Cross School in St. John's, a Brother was telling stories of miracles that he had read in the Bible. At the end of his lesson, he asked if anyone had any questions. A young boy in the class named Dinty, who had a knack for irritating the good Brother raised his hand in response and asked, "What's a miracle?"

The Brother, a little perturbed by the question because he had included an explanation of miracles during the class, answered, "The best way to show you is to demonstrate. Please, Dinty, come up here in front of the class so everyone can see and understand." Dinty strutted up as requested and stood grinning beside the Brother. "Now bend over," the Brother instructed Dinty. Dinty did as the brother had requested. The Brother then lifted his leg and gave Dinty a kick in the arse.

"Did you feel that?" the Brother asked.

"Of course I did, Bro," whimpered Dinty.

"See, Dinty, if you hadn't that would have been a miracle," said the Brother.

### The Jet

A jet plane flew over St. John's. Trapper Gillett commented, "I wish I could go as fast as that."

"You could if your arse was on fire!" said Dinty Hearn.

### Dinty Had the Answer

Brother T. I. Murphy was the most popular Brother at Holy Cross school because his sister owned and operated the famous Power's Candy Story on New Gower Street, west of Springdale Street, and he always had a supply of candy to pass out to his students for good behaviour.

During a class at Holy Cross, Brother Murphy was trying to demonstrate a simple experiment in the generation of steam. "What have I in my hand?" he asked.

"A tin can," replied Larry Mooney.

"Very true. Is the can an animate or inanimate object?" asked Brother Murphy.

"Inanimate," shouted Charlie Fowler.

"Exactly! Now can any boy in this class tell me how, with this can, is it possible to generate a surprising amount of speed and power almost beyond control?" asked Brother Murphy, who by now was pleased with the attentiveness and knowledge of his students. Michael "Dinty" Hearn raised his hand. "You may answer, Dinty," said Brother Murphy.

"Tie it to a dog's tail," answered Dinty

### The York Theatre!

In old St. John's, the bars were not the only places where you could run into a rough time. The following story took place at the York Theatre on Water Street. The boys went there in gangs. Gangs from Cabot Sreet, Flower Hill, Carter's Hill, and so on. When Clar Wheeler first went to work there as an usher, he would strut up and down the aisles with his flashlight, and anyone acting out of the way would be tossed out.

On this day, he shone the flashlight into one of the rows beneath the balcony and saw Dino Caul with his two legs up over the seat in front of him and crouched down into the seat. Clar shouted...."Hey, get your feet off the seat!"

Dino responded with an, "Ahhhhhhhhhhhhhhhh." But he didn't move.

Again Clar shouted, "Get your feet off the seat or I'll throw you out the door."

And again Dino replied, "Ahhhhhhhhhhhhhhhhhhhh."

Obviously irritated because Dino was apparently ignoring him, Clar asked, "Where did you come from?"

Dino looked at Clar and pointing towards the balcony answered, "Th..th..the balcony.....Dinty Hearn threw me over."

## At the York Theatre

Dinty: So you were thrown out of the side exit of the York on your arse. What happened then?

Edward: I told the usher that my father was a prominent St. John's lawyer.

Dinty: So what?

Edward: He apologized and invited me inside again. When I went in, he grabbed me by the shoulder and threw me out the front door.

## Dinty's Thought

On another occasion, Brother Jake Batterton had been combining prophesy with events in the modern world. He posed the question, "What would you say if I were to tell you that in a very short space of time all the rivers of South America and Africa will dry up?"

The class was silent enough to hear Dinty Hearn, who was bored, comment, "I would say, go thou and do likewise!"

## The Air We Breathe

Brother Harry French, at Holy Cross School in St. John's, was trying to get his class to understand the air we breathe. He asked if anyone could identify what pervades all space, something which no wall or door can shut out.

"The smell of boiled cabbage," answered the Dinty Hearn.

## Dinty's Wit

Dinty Hearn used to say about a childhood buddy who had big ears, "When Dickey was growing up his ears were so long his mother used to hide him during rabbit hunting season."

\* \* \*

Whenever Dinty was describing a particular, popular grocery store on New Gower Street in the 1950s he would say, "The cleanest thing in the store was the cat in the window."

\* \* \*

Dinty, collecting door to door for the TB Association, suggested a home owner, "Give 'til it hurts."

"Here's a quarter," she said.

"You can't stand much pain," said Dinty.

\* \* \*

Dinty: "Bessie the Hump once put baking powder on her face and it broke out in biscuits."

\* \* \*

Dinty explaining to Jack Murphy what an AC-DC radio was, "AC means Around the City. DC means Distant Countries."

\* \* \*

Dinty: "Fatso Ryall went salmon fishing and never even caught a can!"

\* \* \*

When Dinty was asked by his brother Pat what was good for biting nails, he answered, "Sharp teeth!"

\* \* \*

Jack Murphy asked Dinty, "What's the difference between the York Theatre and Sunday School?"

Dinty Hearn answered, "In Sunday School they sing "Stand up! Stand Up for Jesus." At the York, they shout, "Sit down! Sit down, for Christ sake!"

## It's Just A Needle

The grade two students at Holy Cross were taken to the basement area in a line-up to receive their polio vaccine. Among the students was Dinty Hearn. The boys were taken two at a time into an office where a doctor and nurse were administering the vaccine. Some kids screamed and cried as they received the needle and this frightened the boys waiting in the hall. Dinty was keeping up a brave front when his name was called. He was met at the door by a doctor with a needle in his hand who tried to assure him there was really nothing to it. The doctor showed Dinty the needle and commented, "Just a little prick with a needle."

"I know you are," said Dinty, "but what are going to do with that?"

### Frank "Toe" Byrne

Toe Byrne was standing outside the elevator at St. Clare's Hospital one day selling old Newfoundland pictures from his briefcase. These were popular items and several staff members had gathered around. Suddenly, an elevator door opened and a doctor, well-known for his English accent said scornfully, "Mister Byrne, this is not the lobby of a hotel."

Toe shot back, "Right, and if you were any f——n good, you would still be in England."

### Mrs. Cooney's Cooking

Toe was a true St. John's wit. He once said that Mrs. Cooney's specialty was making dumplings with the emphasis on "dump." "But everything else she makes would melt in your mouth...it might take a few days, but it will melt."

### Toe Byrne the Critic

Ben Jackman was singing a Newfoundland folk song while having a beer with his buddies at the Belmont. An American soldier at a nearby table asked Toe Byrne, "Is that a popular Newfoundland song he's singing?"

Toe answered, "It was before Ben started singing it!"

### Newfie Bullet

The ticket clerk in the railway office told a passenger that if he ran he could catch the train. Toe Byrne, standing nearby, commented, "If you run, you can pass it."

\* \* \*

Toe Byrne said, "Tommy Toe goes down to the Regatta in the back of a bus and comes back in the back of the Black Mariah." "Police wagon"

### It's Not the Hearing Aid

Brother Hammond was deaf and wore a hearing aid. One day when he had roll call, the boys in class agreed to lip sync their answers to the call. He started, Richard Murphy, and Richard mouthed his name, then Pat Hearn, Charles Fowler and each boy called lip-synced his name. Then we could hear Brother Hammond say, "Oh God, and he fumbled with his hearing aid, turning it up." Each name after that was properly answered and the Brother never learned the difference.

### Religious Class

During a religion class at Holy Cross in St. John's, the Brother asked Trapper Gillett, "Who made you?"

"God made me, Brother," replied Trapper. Trapper then asks for permission to go to the bathroom and then leaves the classroom.

The Brother asks Jimmy Murphy, "Who made you?"

"Adam and Eve," answers Jimmy.

"No," said the Brother, "God made you!"

"No, Brother, Adam and Eve made me. God made Trapper Gillett and he's gone to the bathroom," said Jimmy.

### Lost Vocation

In 1950, Gerry "The Beaver" Murphy of St. John's found himself getting off a bus outside Dublin, Ireland, where he had registered to enter a seminary to study for the priesthood. The bus had stopped at the bottom of a long winding unpaved path that led to a monastery on the top of the hill. The Beaver struggled up the bumpy path carrying a large suitcase which contained all his personal belongings. His foot tripped in a rock and he stumbled ahead almost falling. "Oh shit," he said. Then he stood erect and said, "F- - k, I said shit!" Then he bit his tongue and said, "Shit I said f- - k."

The Beaver went back down the hill carrying his suitcase and got back on board the bus. As he passed by the bus-driver, he commented, "F- - k it, I didn't want to be a priest anyway."

### Out of Toilet Paper

Ben Jackman sent a letter to the Simpson Sears Company asking for the price of toilet paper. He received a reply advising him that he could find the information he needed on page 237 of the Simpson Sears Catalogue. Ben wrote back, "If I had your catalogue, I wouldn't need the toilet paper."

### Avoid Fighting

When little Jackie Murphy ran into his house, his mother asked, "Why is your face all red?"

"I was running up Flower Hill to avoid a fight," replied Jackie.

"That's a nice thing to do. Who was fighting?" asked Mrs. Murphy.

"Me and Dinty Hearn," replied Jackie.

### The Glasgow Ham-bone

Roman Catholics considered eating meat on Friday to be a mortal sin and a matter for confession. During the weekly confessions held at St. Patrick's Church in the west end of St. John's, the pious Kitty Martin stepped into the confession box of Father Murphy.

"Father, I committed a mortal sin," confessed Kitty.

"A mortal sin, go on, please explain," asked Father Murphy.

"Well Father, I had a ham-bone for my dinner on Friday," Kitty confessed.

"Where did you buy the ham-bone?" asked Father Murphy.

"I bought it at Lar Glasgow's on Brazil Square, Father," replied Kitty.

"My child, you didn't commit any mortal sin, sure the whole west end knows that Lar Glasgow doesn't leave any meat on his ham-bones," said Father Murphy.

### The Singing Priest

On another occasion, Kitty Martin confessed to Father Murphy that she had sinned since her last confession. When Father Murphy asked her to explain, she said "Well Father, I am a little embarrassed to tell you this but when you were singing at mass last Sunday, I laughed."

"Now then, that could be a serious offence," said Father Murphy.

"I am very sorry Father," commented Kitty

"Tell me, my child, how much money did you put in the collection plate last Sunday," asked Father Murphy.

"Five cents, Father," answered Kitty.

"Well now, for five cents, who did you expect to hear singing, John McCormack?" asked Father Murphy.

### The Mission

During the men's mission held each season of Lent, St. Patrick's Parish Church in St. John's was filled to capacity. At such a mission in 1950, the mission father's sermon had gone on much longer than the usual sermons. He was going down the long list of prophets and relating each one's importance to our Christian faith. With many more to go, he paused impressively and declared, "And Habbakuk, where shall we put him?"

Doc Butler from Flower Hill, who was bored by the long sermon, stood up in the back row, and as he made his way out exclaimed, "He can have my seat!"

### When Mary Sang

Mrs. Murphy loved to sing old Newfoundland songs while housecleaning. However, as soon as she would start singing, her husband Mike would sit in the window and wave with both hands to neighbours passing on the street. One day Mrs. Murphy asked, "Mike, why is it that every time I sing you go and sit in the window, waving your two hands like a maniac?"

"Well, I want everyone to know that I'm not beating you," replied Mike.

## Temperance Meeting

Temperance meetings were held regularly during the 1950s at the Total Abstinence Society Rooms on Duckworth Street. At a meeting one evening for those trying to kick the habit, Stan Dooley was "on the door." On the door meant he acted as a bouncer in cases when trouble erupted.

The small crowd listened attentively to the speaker whom they found compelling. He questioned the group. "What is it that we all want when we get home, tired from work? What do we long for to lighten our burdens, to gladden our hearts, and to bring a smile of bliss and happiness to our lips?"

When he paused for effect, Stan, who rarely missed the opportunity to act 'the tough guy,' shouted, "And the f-f-first man who says 'a d-d-d-rink' goes out on his arse."

## The Boys and Revival

During the early 1950's, Stan Dooley and Whitey Reardigan dropped in on an old time revival meeting being held in downtown St. John's. The two had been drinking, and Whitey was in a devil of a mood.

The preacher was addressing the gathering and saying: "The Lord is good to me. He giveth me peace. He giveth me happiness. He giveth me wealth. Surely my cup runeth over! What will I do?...What will I do?"

From the back of the hall, Whitey shouted, "Pour it in your saucer."

## The Johnny Coat at the Old General

Jim Fardy, Doc Butler and Stan Dooley made it to the old Fever Hospital in the late 1940s to see a neighbour and friend, Jack Abbott. In those days, if a bad virus was on the go, the hospitals, as now, would demand that you wear one of those white johnny coats and a mask. When they entered the hospital, a nurse passed each of them a Johnny coat and mask. Jim laid his on a chair in the waiting room and told his friend he was going to the bathroom.

When Jim came out, Stan and Doc were gone. Left in a pile in the middle of the floor were two pair shoes, two pair socks, two pair of underwear, two shirts and two coats. Jim looked down the corridor towards Jack's room and there were Doc and Stan, bare-arsed, with their johnny coats standing by Jack's bed.

### No Smoking Signs

Stan Dooley boarded the old Main Line Bus that was being driven by Andy Churchill, one of the best-known drivers at the time. As the bus left the terminal on Freshwater Road, Andy noticed that Stan had lit up a cigarette and was smoking it. "Now Stan, didn't you see the 'No Smoking' sign?"

"As a matter of fact I did, and I saw the one next to it that says 'Wear Maiden-Form Bras.' So I ignored both of them," answered Stan.

### Not Wanted

An old maid from Clifford Street was trying to strike up a relationship with Stan Dooley. One day, when she dropped off a cooked dinner to Stan, she commented, "The way to a man's heart is through his stomach."

"And the way to the street is your feet. Get out and take your dinner with you," Stan said.

### An Insult

After Stan Dooley of Monroe Street had an exchange of words with a Mrs. Buckmaster, she curtly said, "Well...I didn't come here to be insulted."

Stan retorted, "Oh, where do ya usually go?"

### The Ambulance

Whitey Reardigan loved entertaining the boys on the corner of Flower Hill with stories of his experiences on the battlefront during the Korean War. The boys listened, with eyes wide opened in amazement, as Whitey told of how he survived a fierce battle. "The medics came and lifted me up and laid me in the ammunition wagon."

Stan Dooley, who was hanging on to every word said by Whitey, interrupted him to comment, "You must mean ambulance. They wouldn't have put you in an ammunition wagon."

"Your wrong Stan, I was so full of bullets they figured the ammunition wagon was the best place for me," said Whitey.

### Mouldy Face

Stan was staring at a woman with a long nose and missing teeth who was in the line-up at Glasgow's Meat Market on Brazil Square. The woman noticed Stan and said, "Who are you looking at, buddy? Don't you know we are all cut from the same mould?"

"Yeah! But some faces are mouldier than others," said Stan.

### Do What?

Spuds Hartery was married ten years with no kids. He said his sister told him it was because he was stupid. "Nonsense," said the doctor. "It's probably to do with your diet. Or it might be a question of timing. How many times a week do you do it?"

"Do what?" asked Spuds.

### Stan Tested

Stan applied for a job with the police force and he was given an oral test. The Chief asked him, "If you were in a police car and were being chased by a dangerous gang of crooks who were speeding at 80 mph behind you, what would you do?"

Stan didn't hesitate and said, "90."

### Stan's Watch

With a US Base in the city and another at Argentia, the streets of St. John's always had a sprinkling of American soldiers. A soldier, who was boasting to a bunch of the boys on Flower Hill of the merits of his expensive looking watch, irked Stan. Stan had had enough!

"That's nothing, I dropped my watch into the Waterford River two years ago and its still going!" Stan said.

Taken by surprise, the American asked, "What, the same watch?" To which Stan replied, "No, the Waterford River."

## Newfoundlanders in Africa

When Fonce and Harry, two buddies from St. John's, found themselves with an army regiment ready to land in North Africa during World War II, their Commanding Officer instructed them on how to get along with the natives. He said, "Remember, you need to make friends with the natives. No matter what else you do, do not get into any argument with them. If they say Africa is bigger than Newfoundland, agree with them!"

## Beans and Chocolates

At an outing for the old-time Centre Town of St. John's held at Mullowney's Meadow in Mount Pearl, Khak Crotty was dishing out some homemade baked beans she made for the occasion. Stan Dooley, after tasting them said, "Khak, these are just like the ones in the can me mother used to open."

Stan passed Khak a box of chocolates and said, "I know these are your favourites."

Khak opened the box and said, "There's only a half-box here!"

"Yeah!" said Stan, "They're my favourites too."

## Old Plum Pudding!

Stan Dooley: "Mom, I don't like this plum pudding."

Mother: "Oh, don't you. Well, I'll have you know I was making plum pudding before you were born."

Stan: "That explains it. This must be one of them."

## Stan and Joey

On a hot summer's day in the early 1950s, Stan and Joey met Father Power walking along Water Street with his arm in a cast.

Stan asks, "How'd ya break your arm, Father?"

Father Power replies, "Slipped in the bath."

After the priest leaves, Stan asks, "Joe, what's a bath?"

"How do I know, I'm not a Catholic," answers Joe.

## Changes on George Street

Pauline Prowse returned for a visit to St. John's for the first time in forty years. She was taking in the changes to downtown St. John's with her sisters, Beth and Rose. Pauline was impressed by the bars and little outdoor restaurants that had sprung up in the George Street area. In particular, she was amused that people were actually holding liquor and beer glasses in their hands outdoors.

Pauline told her sisters, "The only time we drank outdoors in the 1950s was if there was a fight indoors."

## Stolen Car

In 1963 someone stole Tucker Crotty's new Chevrolet Belair car. Kit Martin, a neighbour, witnessed the theft and rushed over to tell Tucker that she saw everything. Tucker said, "Great! I was just going to call the police. Can you give me a good description of the guy who robbed the car?"

Kitty said, "I can give you better than that. I wrote down the car's license plate number."

## Towny Holiday

In old St. John's, people's idea of a vacation was to sit on someone else's front steps!

## The Front Steps

Before the advent of television, people in old St. John's would sit on their doorsteps on warm summer evenings. Often, friends and neighbors would gather around the steps of one particular house, and pretty soon a party atmosphere prevailed and someone was sure to initiate a sing-a-long. I recall a popular song at such gatherings was *The Shaving Cream Song*. While collecting popular old songs, now long forgotten, I came across the words to that old favourite. At the 1999 Downtown-Flower Hill Reunion, with a packed hall of over five hundred people, Ben Jackman delighted the audience by singing,

## *The Shaving Cream Song*

I have a sad story to tell you
It may hurt your feelings a **bit**,
Last night, when I walked into my bathroom
I stepped in a big pile of... shhhaving cream,
Be nice and clean, shave every day
And you'll always look clean

I think I'll break off with my girlfriend.
Her antics are queer I'll **admit**.
Each time I say "darling, I love you",
She tells me that I'm full of... shhhaving cream,
Be nice and clean, shave every day
And you'll always look clean.

Our baby fell out of the window,
You'd think that her head would be **split**
But good luck was with her that morning
She fell in a barrel of... shhhaving cream,
Be nice and clean, shave every day
And you'll always look clean

An old lady died in a bathtub
She died from a terrible **fit**,
In order to fulfill her wishes
She was buried in six feet of... shhhaving cream,
Be nice and clean, shave every day
And you'll always look clean.

When I was in France with the army
One day I looked into my **kit**
I thought I would find me a sandwich
But the darn thing was loaded with... shhhaving cream
Be nice and clean, Shave everyday
And you'll always look clean

*And now folks my story is ended*
*I think it is time I should **quit**,*
*If any of you feel offended*
*Stick your head in a barrel of... shhhaving cream*
*Be nice and clean, Shave everyday*
*And you'll always look clean*

### Christmas Cake

On Christmas Day, Kitty visited Doc Butler at his home in downtown St. John's with a piece of cake she had baked, and said, "It's made from a recipe handed down in my family from my great grandmother."

"I never eat hand-me-downs," retorted Doc.

"Thank you very much. I feel insulted. I came in here with the Christmas Spirit," said Kitty.

"And the face of Halloween," Doc added. As Kitty stormed out of the house, Doc commented, "Don't drop that cake on your foot, or you'll be crippled for a week."

### The Newfie Bullet

The year was 1952. The Newfie Bullet (as Newfoundland's cross-country train was called) came to a dead stop. Doc Butler, on his way from St. John's to Montreal, was irritated by the delay and asked the conductor, "Why in the name of all that's holy have we stopped in the middle of nowhere?"

"We had to. There was a cow on the tracks," replied the Conductor.

The train crew managed to move the cow from the tracks and the train continued on its journey. Fifteen minutes later, it came to another complete stop, and again in the middle of nowhere.

Doc catches up with the conductor and says, "Good grief, don't tell me we caught up with that cow again."

### Straight Talking Spuds

Spuds Hartery's mother told him to wear clean underwear every day while at the summer Kinsman Camp at Donovans off Topsail Road. After five days, Spuds couldn't button up his pants.

\* \* \*

When Spuds' sister Annie asked him if her new dress made her look big, he answered, "It's not the dress but your big fat arse that makes you look big."

\* \* \*

Annie and her boyfriend Bud would spell out words if Spuds was around when they did not want him to know what they were talking about.

Bud: "Your brother is D-U-M-B!"
Annie: "Yeah, he's a real I-D-I-O-T!"
Bud: "Boy! He even looks S-T-U-P-I-D!"
Spuds: "Listen, if ye don't want to take me to the movies, ye don't have to spell it out!"

## Feet First

Spuds always had a headache after he got out of bed in the morning. His mother would keep reminding him, "Spuds, how often have I told you, when you get out of bed, it's feet first!"

## The Boys at Holy Cross

Jim Casey to Spuds: "Close your eyes and think of a number between one and twenty."
Spuds: "Yep!"
Casey: "Now double it, add two and subtract seventeen."
Spuds: "Yep!"
Casey: "Now subtract the number you started with"
Spuds: "Yep!"
Casey: "Dark, ain't it?"

## On Stage with Spuds

"Now Spuds," said Mr. Conway, who was producing a play for the Holy Cross Spring concert, "do you think you could manage to take on the part of the village constable? The man is supposed to be a dull and stupid idiot, so the role will suit you down to the ground. All you have to say when the gun is fired by the villain is, 'My God, it's gunfire!' You have no other words at all. Think you can manage it?"

"Yep, I can handle it," said Spuds, so home he went, and for weeks he rehearsed the tragic words to himself, "My God, it's gunfire!" He dreamt of them and sometimes woke up screaming, thinking a gun had really gone off. He attended rehearsals most religiously, but the 'starter' gun was never actually fired. A sharp knock on the wall sufficed and then Spuds would shout out his lines.

The night of the concert came, the auditorium was filled, and as was the custom, His Grace, the Archbishop, was seated in the front row with other prominent guests. Spuds stood in the wings petrified with stage fright. Then he entered on cue. The sharp and constrained crash of the gun resounded upon his ears.

"Jesus, Mary and Joseph," he shouted, rushing on stage, "what's that?"

### Shocking Language!

The parish priest was on McFarlane Street collecting the annual church dues. A young boy named Max, while hammering nails into the wooden steps in front of his house, struck his finger with the hammer and let go with a string of obscenities that would curl a sailor's hair. The priest, who was about to enter the house at the time, was shocked and admonished at little Max saying, "Watch your language, young man!" Max quickly replied, "English Father, what's yours?"

### First Plane Ride

When Beth Kearsey took her first ride on an airplane, the stewardess asked if she wanted a seat by the aisle, or the window.

Beth answered, "By the aisle. I can't sit near the window, I just had my hair done."

### Shoes Didn't Fit

A fellow went into Parker and Monroe's on Water Street and complained, "These shoes you sold me don't fit. One of them has a heel two inches shorter than the other. What am I supposed to do?"

"Limp!" replied the clerk.

### The Coal Wagon

During the late 1940s, Chick Carey was a wagon-driver for the Newfoundland Coal Company. One day, while the horse-drawn wagon made its way up Flower Hill with a delivery for the Upper Levels, Harry Murphy noticed the great effort made by the horse. He watched Chick shaking the reigns and heard him hollering, "Giddy up, Bessie! Come on Dobbin! Giddy up Queenie! Get'er moving Trigger!"

Harry asked Chick, "Why has the old mare got so many names?"

"Shhhh!" said Chick. "Her name is 'Betsy,' but when she got the blinders on her, and I yell all those other names, she thinks she's got all those horses helping her."

### Smart Widow

Old Ned Ryan had passed away and was waking in the parlor of his home in downtown St. John's. A mourner stepped up near the coffin and said, "Poor Ned, he's feeling no pain now. What did he die of?"

"He died of the gonorrhea," the widow answered.

A close neighbor then stepped alongside the widow and said, "Poor soul! He looks so peaceful. What took him, maid?"

"Yes, he's at peace now, poor-fella, he died of the gonorrhea," said the widow.

Suddenly, Ned Jr. called his mother aside and said, "Mom, that's an awful thing your saying about dad. He didn't die of gonorrhea. He died of diarrhea!"

"Sure, I know that," said the widow Ryan. "But I would rather have people thinkin' he died like a sport, instead of the shit that he was!"

### She Made It!

When poor old Kit Martin went to St. Clare's for an operation, she woke up in her room with the curtains closed. She asked the Doctor why the curtains were closed, and he explained, "There's a big fire across the street and I didn't want you to think you hadn't made it."

### Miracle?
A thunder storm was raging outside St. Patrick's Church as Father Bradshaw was reading from the book of Job. "Yea, the light of the wicked shall be put out." Lightning struck an outside transformer and the church was thrown into total darkness.

### Wedding Colours
Attending a wedding at St. Patrick's Church in St. John's for the first time, Dolores Murphy asks her mother, "Why is the bride dressed in white?"

Her mother tries to explain it in simple terms and says, "Because white is the colour of happiness and today is the happiest day of her life."

Dolores was quiet for a moment and then asked, "Well, why is the groom wearing black."

### Outport Girl at Wedding
This story was popular at St. John's weddings during the 1940s and 1950s. The master of ceremonies would pose the question, "How can you tell an outport girl at a wedding?"

Then he would answer, "She's the one wearing something old, something new, something borrowed, something blue." He would then hesitate and continue, "something red, something orange, something brown, something purple, something yellow," until he ran out of colours.

### King of the House
Paddy ordered his wife to go to the corner store and pick him up a package of cigarettes and a half dozen Haig Ale.

"What do I get?" his wife asked.

"You get to stay in one piece," replied Paddy.

### Mundy Pond Bus
During the early 1950s, hundreds of downtown St. John's families moved to new subsidized housing units in the Ebsary Estates area (Cashin Avenue). At that time, Mundy Pond seemed to be a

long haul from the centre of the old City and the Capitol Coach Line Bus Company operated a bus to connect downtown with the Mundy Pond Area. In fact, the bus was called the Mundy Pond. One of the families to make the move was the Evans family.

Mrs. Evans took with her the family cat 'Cisco', who had been with them for almost a decade. The Housing Authority had a regulation forbidding keeping pets in the apartment, so when Cisco passed away under the kitchen stove one night, Mrs. Evans was relieved. Because the Housing Inspector was due to visit the next day, Mrs. Evans told her eldest son Alex to wrap the cat in brown paper and instructed him to take it with him on the Mundy Pond Bus on his way to Holy Cross. He was told to throw the package from the window into the first clearing the bus came to.

Allan boarded the bus and placed the package on the seat alongside him while awaiting the opportunity to toss it through the window. When Boo Kennedy came and sat beside him, the two became engrossed in a conversation and Alex completely forgot about the dead cat. When time came to leave the bus, Alex had to take the package to school with him. He thought he would get rid of it on his way home in the afternoon, so he hid the package in the bathroom at school.

In the afternoon, after retrieving the brown wrapped package, Alex boarded the bus and sat next to a window at the rear. He was determined not to forget his mother's orders as he again placed the package alongside him on the seat. By then, it was after 4:00 p.m. and people were returning home with packages picked up from a shopping trip to the downtown business section. On this occasion, a middle-age lady sat next to him with packages of her own.

Alex was in a sweat. "How in God's good name can I dump the cat now?" he asked himself. Finally, the bus reached Alex's stop. Quick as a wink, Alex contrived a scheme to rid himself of the cat. He figured, "I'll just leave the package on the bus and get off. Who'll notice? And I'll be rid of the cat once and for all!"

But when Alex was halfway down the aisle the lady shouted, "Come back young fella, you forgot your parcel."

Now Alex was pissed, but there was little he could do. He pretended to be surprised and gracefully accepted the package while thanking the lady for not allowing him to forget it. Mrs. Evans was livid when Alex walked into the kitchen with the cat still in his possession. After giving him the scolding of his life, she said, "Give me the package and I'll burn it in the furnace." But as she seized the package, it fell open onto the floor and, 'lo and behold,' there was one of the finest hams ever to come from Casey's Butcher Shop.

Alex had one of the great stories of old St. John's to remember, but not likely as intriguing as the one the lady, who was left with the dead cat had to tell.

### Dirty Towel

Ben Jackman, while walking past the old Brownsdale Hotel in downtown St. John's, told his buddy "Gog" Abbott, "I don't know what they wash the towels with in there, but I was there once and dropped a towel on the floor and it broke."

### Mixed Signals

Mary Murphy of Flower Hill had planned to tune into Gerry Wiggins on CJON at 3:30 p.m. one afternoon to take notes on a recipe she wanted. Something unexpected came up and she told her daughter Beth to listen to the program and write down the recipe. Beth wouldn't think of saying no to her mother's request. However, at the same time, there was an exercise program being broadcast on VOCM that she really wanted to hear.

Beth felt she could handle the situation by hooking a spare radio up in the kitchen and turning on both programs at the same time. She was confident she could get the recipe and listen to the exercise instructions at the same time. Her mother arrived home at 5:30 and Beth passed her the recipe.

Later that evening when the children were in bed, Mary read Beth's notes:

> *Hands on hips, place one cup of flour on your shoulder, raise knees and depress toes, mix thoroughly in one half cup of orange juice and repeat eight times. Inhale a teaspoon full of baking powder, bend your legs and break two eggs in a measuring cup, exhale — breath naturally and sit in a large bowl.*

*Add one cup of sugar and lie flat on the floor rolling in the whites of two eggs over and over again until it comes to a boil. Place in oven for thirty minutes, remove and brush lightly with your right foot. Breath naturally, dress in shorts after pouring a can of tomato sauce over your hips. Serves four people.*

### Bridie Cole

Bridie Cole, a loveable character and wit of old St. John's, turned up at a downtown wedding after being out of circulation for years. When Bridie was asked by the host how her health was, she put her two hands to her face and answered, "Thank God wrinkles don't hurt."

Bridie would never tell her age. When asked how old she was, she would answer, "If I was wine, I'd be worth a fortune."

### Higgins the Lawyer

When Jimmy Higgins was a young lawyer in St. John's, a truck owner came into his office seeking legal advice. After he completed telling every detail of his legal problem, Higgins commented, "Wow! You have got the strongest case I have ever heard."

The trucker put on his hat, expressed his thanks to Jimmy Higgins and started to walk out the door.

"Why are you leaving?" asked a surprised Higgins.

"To settle this case out of court," replied the trucker.

"But I just told you, you have the best case I've ever heard," said Higgins.

"That's possible," said the trucker, "but not for me. I just told you the other fellow's story."

### Fish 'n' Chips and More

A man from Trinity, who had far too much to drink at the old Belmont on New Gower Street in St. John's, got a cab to take him to his boarding house. He strikes up a conversation with the driver who provides an attentive ear. The drunk then leans over the front seat and asks the cabby, "Buddy, have you got enough room

in the front seat for fish 'n' chips and a dozen beer?"
"Yeah, why not?" replied the cabby.
"Thanks buddy," says the drunk as he leans over the front seat and throws up.

### Bob McLeod

One of the immediate benefits of Newfoundland joining with Canada in 1949 was the Baby Bonus. This federal program paid a monthly allowance of six dollars for each child in a family. Bob McLeod, a famous radio personality and popular after dinner speaker, gave the program another name for which it became widely known throughout the province for decades. McLeod referred to the baby bonus as the "Dickey Dole."

### How did we do it?

A school teacher was giving a lesson to his class on the importance of oxygen to the life of human beings, animals and plants. "Oxygen," he said, "is essential to all animal existence. There could be no life without it. Yet, strange to say, it was discovered little more than a century ago."

One bright student then asked, "What did they do, sir, before it was discovered?"

### Three Nationalities

An American, a Frenchman and a Newfoundlander were discussing what each would do if he awoke one morning and discovered he was a millionaire. The Frenchman said he would build himself a huge hockey rink. The American said he would travel around the world and enjoy himself.

The Newfoundlander said he would go back to sleep to see if he could make another million.

### The New Car

*Daddy bought a little car*
*He fed it gasoline,*
*And everywhere that daddy went,*
*He walked. Our son's eighteen!*

### Mom's Recipe

*You may talk about your chicken or ducks or turkey meat,*
*There's another kind of meal my children like to eat.*
*You makes it out o' leavins' most any kind o' trash,*
*And there you have the makings of first class corn-beef hash.*

### Chinese Laundry

Pre-confederation St. John's saw a Chinese Laundry in almost every neighborhood. For ten cents you could get a shirt cleaned and the collar and cuffs starched. People were always amazed over how the laundry men could take in so many white shirts and always deliver them back to the right owner.

A laundryman named Joey went around the homes below LeMarchant Road with a small homemade covered wagon pulled by a horse. At each customer's house, he would take a load of shirts and put them in a large blue bag. He would write something in Chinese on a receipt paper and attach it to the bag. People were amazed that he never got the shirts mixed up. One day, Snoz McGrath, an old gentleman who lived on Wickford Street, (Livingstone Street today) went to the laundry to pick up his shirts and upon receiving them noticed the attached paper with Chinese figures. Pointing to the lettering he asked, "That's my name, I suppose?"

"No," said Joey, "that's 'scliption'."

"Scliption," repeated Snoz. "What do that mean?"

"Scliption says Li'l ol' man. Closs-eyed, no teeth, big nose!" Joey replied.

### The Witty Yetman Brothers

Silly Willy was a character around St. John's from the 1930s to the early 1960s when he passed away. Willy was unable to speak. He wore a long, black overcoat and a salt and pepper hat in all kinds of weather. Willy lived with his father and sister in the family home on Cabot Street. His father was manager of the York Theatre on Water Street.

Willy spent his days wandering city streets. Young children were afraid of him and would run for shelter when they saw him or heard he was in the neighbourhood. Although he was considered harmless, he sometimes chastised younger children by slapping their faces. This would get him in trouble with parents or older brothers and sisters who would shout at him and chase him away.

Willy loved attending funerals. If one passed by while he was walking along a street, he would immediately step in front of the hearse and stay with the procession until he became tired, or was chased away by the threat of the undertaker's whip. He was known by everyone in town and generally treated kindly and generously. Poor Willy once attended a funeral on James Street, at which the Yetman brothers, Bern and Kev, were present. The brothers were known around town for their wit, and were especially welcome at house-wakes because they lifted the spirits of the mourners, and had the Irish touch of turning tears to laughter.

This particular wake was taking place in mid-summer when temperatures were very hot, and it was not at all uncommon to see bugs appear in a casket in some of the older homes especially during this period. When Silly Willy entered and stepped smartly to the side of the casket, the room became very quite. The Yetman brothers stepped near the casket, and one distracted Willy while the other tossed brown rice into the coffin and shouted, 'Maggotts.' Some ladies standing nearby began screaming and were the first behind poor Willy in running from the house.

In the kitchen, the response was simply, "What have the Yetman's done now?" The wake continued, and the story was added to the many anecdotes from old St. John's involving the witty Yetman brothers.

### Fitting Eulogy

Barney Snow was a longshoreman in old St. John's who had very few friends. At his wake, Kitty, the neighbourhood mourner, led those present in the rosary. When the prayers ended, she asked if anyone wished to recall fond memories of Barney. There was no reply. Again Kitty invited someone to pay tribute to Barney's memory adding, "We should be willing to forgive and forget at a time like this."

A silent few minutes passed and Bern Yetman stood up and said, "I'll say something."

"Praise the lord," said Kitty. "Go ahead, my son, Speak!"

Bern looked down into the coffin and in a solemn voice said, "His brother was twice as bad."

### Pete: He Hit First

This practical joke took a little preparation. Pete Yetman would stand by the coffin and his brother Kev would stand nearby. Pete would pretend to strike the deceased, which would be accompanied by the sound of a hand striking flesh, as Pete actually struck his own hand. Mourners would be horrified. Kev would then grab Pete by the shoulder and say, "You SOB, why did you do that?"

"He hit me first," Pete would answer.

This was followed by an instantaneous round of laughter. That's the way old-time wakes were.

### Ancestral Tree

At an old-time wake on Springdale Street, Ambrose and Paddy were discussing the subject of ancestors. Bern and Kev Yetman were sitting nearby listening to the conversation. Paddy said proudly, "I can trace my family tree back more than two hundred years."

Bern couldn't resist commenting, "Only two things live in trees, monkeys and birds, and I don't see any feathers on you."

"Well, Bern, how far back do your family records go?" Paddy asked.

Before Bern could answer, Kev interjected, "Ours were lost in the Flood!"

### Kev Yetman's Favourite Joke

No Yetman-attended wake in old St. John's would be complete without Kev Yetman telling the following story. Father Murphy, the new priest at St. Patrick's Parish, was assigned the unpleasant duty of informing a parishioner of the accidental death of her husband. When he came face to face with the man's wife, he was still struggling as to how to break the sad news. He said, "I'm sorry m'am but your husband's new watch is all broken."

"His watch is all broken, how did that happen?" she asked.

"A piano fell on him," replied Father Murphy.

### Bern Yetman's Favourite

The following joke was the favourite of Bern Yetman. Peter worked late one night and ended up driving his secretary home. She invited him in for a cup of tea. He looked at his watch, and said, "Why not, it's early and the wife is gone to a church meeting." They had a cup of tea, then a few drinks of wine. One thing lead to another and they ended up in bed together.

Time passed quickly, and when Peter looked at his watch, he realized he had stayed much longer than expected. He said, "My gawd, it's 11:30, I better get home!" Peter grabbed his coat in a rush and asked his secretary if she had some talcum powder, which she quickly provided. Peter then rubbed his hands with the powder and rushed home. The minute he walked in the house, he found his wife waiting for him. She demanded to know why he was so late. Peter decided to tell the truth, that he was at his secretary's house, had a few drinks and ended up in bed. His wife reacted by demanding that he show her his hands, but he refused and put them behind his back.

"I insist on seeing your hands!" she said.

He reluctantly put both hands forward. She inspected them closely and in a loud, angry voice said, "You son of a bitch, you've been bowling again."

### Pete Yetman's Favourite Joke

"Salt Water Bill" and "Here's Me Head, Me Arse is Coming" were two characters of St. John's in the 1950s. They were chatting at Jim Fardy's store on Flower Hill one day when Here's Me Head told Salt Water Bill, "When I die I want a bottle of Newfoundland Screech poured over me grave."

"I'll do that for ya," said Salt Water Bill, but would you mind if it passes through me kidney's first?"

### Irish Wake

The wife of an old fisherman from the Southern Shore had passed away and friends and relatives came to the house-wake from all over the Avalon Peninsula. It was a real Irish wake with whiskey flowing, and singing and laughing. On the morning of the funeral, Paddy, the husband, told his friends, "If ye think there'll be a lot of fun in it, I'll keep her another day!"

### "Ginger" Power

People from St. John's to Cape St. Mary's avoided "Ginger" Power because he smelled like an open sewer. Ginger was so notorious that two fellows in a bar at Trepassey made a bet involving who smelled worst, "Ginger" or an old billy goat. The prize money was held by the bartender while a demonstration was arranged. In short time, a goat was located and brought into the bar, and the bartender fainted. "Ginger" was then brought in, and the goat fainted!

### Corned Beef and Cabbage to die for

Paddy O'Brien lay dying in his bed when the aroma of corned beef and cabbage being cooked by his wife brought a smile to his face. He reached for his wife's hand and said, "Ah darlin', I can leave this world a happy man. Give me a small plate of the Jiggs Dinner you're cookin'!"

"My lord," replied Mrs. O'Brien, "I can't give you any of that. Sure I'm saving that for the wake."

### The Devil in the Graveyard

Late one night, Pat and Mick were passing by the gate of Mount Carmel Cemetery on their way home to Torbay Road. Pat had a gimp leg since birth while his buddy Mick had a hump on his back. Mick suggested they take a short cut through the cemetery. "Not on your life, that place is haunted," replied Pat.

Mick hesitated a moment and said, "I don't believe in ghosts, I'm going in, and I'll be home long before you."

Half way through the graveyard, Mick heard a strange sound and stopped to look around. Suddenly, from behind a large tombstone, the devil himself appeared. Startled, Mick asked, "Who are you?"

"I am the devil, but there's no need to fear me," replied the dark shadowy figure.

After sizing up Mick, Satan said, "What's that you got on your back?"

"That's a hump, I was born with it," answered Mick.

The devil snapped his fingers and the hump disappeared, and so did the devil.

When Pat and Mick met the next day, Pat was amazed to see that the hump on Mick's back was no longer there. Mick explained what had happened, adding that the devil wasn't such a bad guy after all.

Pat commented to Mick, "If the devil could remove the hump off your back, he could cure my gimpy leg."

That night, Pat, all alone, entered the cemetery and began following the same path that Mick had taken. He was prepared when the devil made his sudden appearance from behind the same large tombstone. "I know who you are, Mick told me all about you," said Pat.

The devil stepped closer and began sizing up Pat. He then asked, "What's that you got on your back?"

"Nothing," answered Pat.

The devil snapped his finger and said, "Here, have a hump." Then he disappeared.

## Three Chairs

When Ned Hickey passed away, a funeral mass was held at St. Patrick's Church in St. John's. Ned left a wife and two daughters. In those days, everyone knew everyone else in the city. If you didn't know a person by name, you knew them by sight. The Hickeys were very well-liked and on the day of the funeral, St. Patrick's Church was filled to capacity. Celebrating the funeral mass were Father Power and Father Bradshaw. Father Power was a very gentle, soft-spoken man, whose tone of voice was a couple of decibels above a whisper. Father Bradshaw was hard of hearing and spoke loudly. Most people didn't like going to Father Bradshaw for confession because you were expected to talk louder than usual. It was easy to hear the confessional conversation outside the confessional box.

Well, after everyone had taken their seats, Father Power noticed that Mrs. Hickey and her two daughters had just entered the church walking behind the casket. He looked around the church and determined that there were no vacant seats. He leaned a little towards Father Bradshaw and whispered, "Get three chairs for the Hickeys."

"What did you say, Father?" asked Father Bradshaw.

Speaking a little louder, Father Power again asked, "Get three chairs for the Hickeys."

"I'm sorry, you'll have to speak up, Father, I can't hear you." answered Father Bradshaw.

Irritated by his failure to move Father Bradshaw to action, Father Power took a deep breath and in his loudest voice shouted towards Father Bradshaw, "Three ... chairs...for the Hickeys."

Everyone in church stood up and responded, "Hip! hip! hooray! Hip! hip! hooray!"[1]

## Autopsy

Prosecutor: Doctor, when did you perform the autopsy on the victim?

Doctor: At 10:15 a.m., Tuesday, June 6th.

Prosecutor: And he was dead at the time?

Doctor: No. He was just lying there and wondering why I was performing an autopsy.

## From Gosse's Tavern Window

Dickey Pittman, Skinny O'Neill and Spuds Murphy, all Roman Catholics, were having a few beers at Gosse's Tavern and looking out through the window at the bustling activity along New Gower

---

1. This story was taken from *Another Time, Another Place*, Jack Fitzgerald, Creative Publishers.

Street. They watched people going in and out of a house of ill-repute across the street. A well-known city lawyer came out, and Dickey commented, "I told ya, that man has the morals of an alley cat."

The next person to come out was an Anglican minister. Spuds Murphy observed, "He'll burn in hell."

A short while later their own parish priest came out, and Skinny O'Neill spoke up and said, "There must be somebody sick in the house."

### Power's Candy Store

Agnes Baird frequented Power's Candy Shop on New Gower Street. "What flavors of ice cream do you have?" she asked Fatty Power, who was serving behind the counter.

"We have vanilla, chocolate and blueberry," answered Fatty in a very hoarse voice.

Sympathizing with Fatty's condition, Mrs. Baird asked, "Do you have laryngitis?"

"No," Fatty croaked, "just vanilla, chocolate and blueberry."

### The Wit of Tom Keefe

Tom Keefe of Tilting Harbour, Fogo, was a popular wit in the area during the days before Confederation. Tom used to deal with John W. Hodge, a merchant at Fogo. One spring, Tom Keefe rowed up to Fogo as usual to pick up his supplies to go fishing. He was in a hurry and did not want to lose time in getting the supplies. Unfortunately for Tom, when he arrived, the general store was filled with fishermen picking up their supplies and they were in just as much a hurry as he was. Tom pushed and elbowed his way through the crowd until he got to the counter and began telling the merchant, Tom Hodge, what he needed.

"Look here, Tom, don't be in such a fret, man, the world wasn't made in a day you know!" said Mr. Hodge.

Even Mr. Hodge broke into laughter when Tom flashed back, "No, sir, that it wasn't. No, there's at least a week's work on it yet!"

## "Cranack's"

The word "cranack" was commonly used throughout Newfoundland prior to Confederation. Cranacks were sought after in summer because they made "a fierce heat" for cooking. The word cranack refers to short ends of dry wood that people used to go into the woods and bring out tied up in bundles on their backs. Simply put, "cranacks" are broken off alder sticks, small birches, etc. that have become white and bone dry.

The term "spell" was another word common in those days, but had another meaning for many Newfoundlanders. It meant to carry.

During the 1940s, a young teacher from St. John's named Miss Fox accepted a teaching position at Western Bay, Conception Bay North. One day, one of her pupils was absent from school, and when he returned the next day, she demanded an explanation for his absence the day before. He told her that he had been "spelling cranacks" all day.

"Spelling cranacks?" she repeated. "And can you spell it now?"

Amid the laughter of the whole class, who saw immediately that the teacher had no idea of the meaning of "cranack," or "spelling" in the context stated by the student, the boy replied, "Yes, ma'am, I can spell cranacks on my back."

## Flour Barrelled Money

A Welfare Officer, who was advising a family head on how not to squander his money, asked his client where he banked his money. The client answered, "We don't use a bank."

"Well, what do you do with the money?" the Officer asked.

"Well, I pays me rent, pays me light and phone bills, then pays me other bills. Then we buys a month's groceries and puts children's lunch money away. And whatever we got left, we stores in a flour barrel in the kitchen."

## Slick Lawyer

An accountant with a large merchant firm in St. John's was facing charges of embezzlement and a lengthy jail term if found guilty. He met with his lawyer on Duckworth Street. After hearing his client's story, the lawyer told him to remain calm, "I can easily handle this. I'll show the jury that you did not have access to the funds that were stolen. I'll get a doctor or two to say that you were temporarily insane. I'll pay off a couple of witnesses and I'll have a cousin on the jury. The judge, by the way, is a very good friend of mine. Meanwhile, I think you should try to escape!

### Fast Horse

A farmer from Topsail was in St. John's looking to buy a horse. "Boy, I got just the horse for you," said old Fitzpatrick. "He's seven years old, sound as a dollar and goes twelve miles without stopping."

"Naw, he's no good fer me," said the farmer. "I live ten miles from town and if I had that horse I'd have to walk back two miles."

### Sunlight Soap Cleans Everything!

Soon after the introduction of the radio to Newfoundland, a burglar broke into the home of a prominent merchant living in the east end of St. John's. Late at night, and with the house in total darkness, the burglar made his way along the wall, reached out to a knob, twisted it slowly, and listened to hear the tumblers click. Instead he heard, "...Clean your hands, hair, floor and sink with Sunlight Soap, the soap that cleans everything."

### Duck Hunter

A fellow from St. John's was returning home with an empty bag from a day's hunting along the Southern Shore. He passed a farm near Bay Bulls with a bunch of ducks swimming in a small pond. "How much will ya charge to let me take a few shots at the ducks?" the townie asked.

"Five dollars," answered the farmer.

The townie fired his gun and killed eight ducks. He paid the farmer the five dollars. "Well, I got the best of that bargain," said the townie.

"I don't give a damn," said the farmer, "they're not my ducks and that's not my pond." He then boarded his tractor and sped away, just as the two hefty-sized owners came running across the field.

## Little Willie

*Little Willie hung his sister;*
*She was dead before we missed her.*
*Willie's always up to tricks.*
*Ain't he cute? He's only six.*

## Calm Down Father Murphy!

Paddy O'Brien went through a stop sign and sent headlong into a car driven by Father Murphy. The priest's car was struck with such force that he spun around several times before crashing against a wrought iron fence. Father Murphy, although badly shaken, was not seriously injured. Paddy jumped out of his car and rushed to the aid of Father Murphy.

"Are you hurt, Father? It was all my fault, I'm terribly sorry," said Paddy.

"Blessed Mother, Paddy," said Father Murphy, "you could have killed both of us!"

"I know Father, I am so sorry. Here, have a drop of the sacramental Newfoundland Screech. It will calm your nerves and make you feel a lot better," said Paddy.

Father Murphy took a couple of swigs from the bottle and berated Paddy, "What in the name of all that's holy, Patrick, were you thinkin' about. You nearly launched me into eternity, for sure."

"Father Murphy, I am really sorry," said Paddy. "Here, take another drop of the 'National,' it'll calm your nerves."

The two talked about the accident and when the bottle was nearly empty, Father Murphy asked, "Paddy, why don't you have a drink?"

"No thanks, Father," Paddy said, "I'll just sit here with you and wait, I want to be sober when the police arrive."

## Lady Needs New Maid

The lady of the house was interviewing her new maid: "Oh yes, Annie," she added, "I forgot to ask you if you had any religious views?"

Young Annie smiled and replied sweetly, "No, ma'am, I haven't.

But I've got some wonderful snapshots of Quidi Vidi Lake and Bowring Park."

## The Psychiatrist and the Lady

The fashionable psychiatrist finished his notes and turned to the lady in front of him. "I'll be perfectly frank," he said. "I find nothing the matter, nothing abnormal, and I shall so inform your relatives."

"Thank you, doctor, I was sure you'd say that," she replied. "I only came here to please my family. After all, there's nothing very strange about a fondness for pancakes, is there?"

"Pancakes?" repeated the psychiatrist. "Certainly not. I'm fond of them myself."

"Are you?" she asked enthusiastically. "Then you must come over to my house. I have trunks full of them!"

## Tobacco

*Tobacco is a filthy weed,*
*I like it!*
*It satisfies no normal need,*
*I like it!*
*It makes you thin, it makes you lean,*
*It takes the hair right off your bean,*
*It's the worst darned stuff I've ever seen..*
*I like it!*

## Newspaper Bloopers

"Most people know the position taken by the present incumbent. But where will he stand when he takes his seat?"

\* \* \*

"Having broken both legs in a collision, Betsy Power is recovering under the car of Dr. Tolson Smith."

\* \* \*

An advertisement in St. John's newspapers promoting the sale of newly arrived-washing machines: "Don't kill your wife. Let our washing machine do the dirty work."

\* \* \*

"Bumper Neil is in the General Hospital. He is suffering from head injuries and shock caused by coming into contact with a live wife."

\* \* \*

"The Legion of Mary Ladies Association held a bazaar last night at the St. Patrick's Parish Hall. Every member had brought something they no longer needed. Many ladies brought their husbands."

\* \* \*

"Three shots rang out. Two of the passengers fell dead; the other went through his hat."

## Answers on School Tests

The Papal Bull was really a cow that was kept at the Vatican to supply milk for the Pope's children.

\* \* \*

The letters M. D. means, "Mentally Deficient."

\* \* \*

A millennium is something like a centennial, only it has more legs.

\* \* \*

Capital punishment should not be used in schools.

\* \* \*

Our forefathers are not living as long as they did.

\* \* \*

Mushrooms look like umbrellas because they always grow in damp places.

\* \* \*

During the Napoleonic Wars, crowned heads were trembling in their shoes.

\* \* \*

A bamboo is an Italian baby.

## The Piano Player

A Gower Street man was bragging to his neighbour, "My daughter can do anything with the piano."

"Can she lock it up and throw the key in St. John's Harbour," inquired the neighbor.

### The Jaywalker

Tommy Toe was walking in front of J.M. Devine's "Big Six" store at the western corner of Bishop's Cove and Water Street when he spotted his buddies on the opposite side near the General Post Office. He shouted, "Wait for me, boys!" and began running across the street.

Constable Stapleton saw him and shouted, "Tommy! What did I tell you about jaywalking?"

Tommy stopped dead in his tracks and looked back towards the constable and shouted, "Well, take me shoes!"

### The Wine Expert!

"When it comes to wine, I'm the expert," Tommy Toe bragged to his friends at a gathering behind the old General Post Office on Water Street.

"Well, what makes you the wine expert?" asked Cuz, another city character.

"You just give me a drink of wine and not only will I tell you the year it was made, I'll tell ya who jumped on the grapes!" answered Tommy.

### Must be Courtin!

Bessie said to her husband, "Georgie, you must have a girlfriend!"

"I certainly do not," said Georgie.

"You gotta have one, because you've washed your feet three times this week," said Bessie.

### Saves Money!

Jim Byrne was a well-known businessman of old St. John's who was famous for his thriftiness. He pointed out to friends a way of saving money when painting around the house. He would say, "Don't waste good paint!"

He explained, "Paint always collects in the indented rim of a paint can, flows down the outside and is wasted. Punch two small nail holes in the rim, and the paint will run back into the can again.

Another thrifty idea he suggested, tongue in cheek, to friends was, when moving residence, scrape the wallpaper off the wall and use it at your new residence. Jim would add, "And, you know, there was a fella I told that to who really tried it."

### The Golfer and the Devil

A golfer found himself at the gates to the great beyond in the afterworld. He was met by the devil and his welcoming committee. "We're always glad to have another golfer," said the devil. "You'll find our local course is a golfer's dream. But come and see for yourself."

With that, the devil led the golfer through the luxurious clubhouse complete with resplendent lounge and lavish cocktail bar. They then visited the ultra-modern locker room containing both shower and bath facilities. "Now for the course itself," said the devil. The golfer was overjoyed to see the well-treed fairways and greens of smoothly-textured grass and the well-kept sand traps. He decided to have a game immediately. He was handed the finest golf bag he had ever seen, containing beautifully-matched sets of woods and irons. "Gosh," he thought, "this isn't such a bad place after all." He pulled out the driver, walked to the first tee, and asked the devil for a ball.

"Oh," said the devil musingly, "THAT'S the hell of it. No golfballs!"

### Planting Potatoes

A man named Mick from Codroy on Newfoundland's west coast was doing time at the Penitentiary in St. John's for embezzling a large amount of money from his employer. His wife wrote him a letter complaining, "It's time to plant the potatoes and I'm going to have to dig up the garden myself."

Mick wrote back, "Don't dig up the garden, that's where I hid the money." Letters leaving the prison were censored and when Mick's letter was read it was passed over to police.

A few days later a dozen policemen arrived at Mick's house and dug up the garden in search of the money. Mick's wife sent off another letter to him complaining, "The police came and dug up the entire garden, what will I do?"

Mick responded, "Plant the potatoes!"

### Me Old Age Pension?

The dear old lady wasn't feeling so good, so she went to see her doctor. He examined her, told her there was nothing seriously wrong with her, but thought she could use a tonic. "Here's a prescription," he said, "get your druggist to fill it. It'll make you ten years younger."

"Oh my Jasus," replied the old lady, "if it makes me ten years younger, what about me old age pension?"

### An Important Hammer

During a drilling operation in Newfoundland waters during the late 1960s, a fellow from Avondale dropped a hammer down the shaft. This resulted in all drilling being stopped for days on end until, finally, it was removed. It must have cost the oil company a fortune. The manager called all the workers together and requested that the Avondale man step forward. He presented him with the hammer.

"I want you to accept this as a memento and hope it will always remind you of the trouble and money you caused this company through your carelessness. So take it and f—k off, you're fired."

"You mean, I'm fired," asked the worker.

"Exactly," replied the boss.

"Well this hammer is no f–ing good to me." As he walked away, he dropped it down the shaft and left the project manager dumbfounded.

### The Farmer

A farmer from Bay Bulls had a very large hay farm. His son, Micky, hated farm work and decided to move into St. John's where the only job he could find was shining shoes. Now the farmer makes hay while the son shines.

### Clean Breakfast

Mrs. Murphy gave her husband soap flakes instead of cornflakes for breakfast. "Was he mad?" Mrs. Fowler asked.

"He certainly was. He foamed from the mouth," Mrs. Murphy replied.

### Combined Problems

What do you get when you cross an insomniac, an agnostic and a dyslexic?

A person who stays awake all night wondering if there really is a **DOG**.

### Good Work

"Are you positive," demanded defence lawyer Higgins, "that the prisoner is the man who stole your car?"

"Well, I was until you cross-examined me. Now, I'm not sure I even had a car."

### Luck

George, an old fisherman, was on his deathbed. He asked his wife Mary to move closer. "Me love, you were with me when we had nothing, and had to get by on the six-cent a day dole. But we did it, didn't we?"

"That we did," replied Mary.

"Remember when I started fishing and we were out in Freshwater Bay when the high waves swamped the boat. We were lucky to make it to shore. But you were with me, Mary, you were with me," said George.

"That I was," answered Mary. "That I was."

"Remember when our first house burnt to the ground and we got out with nothing but the clothes on our backs. But you were there, Mary, you were with me," said George.

"Yes, George me love, I was with you," said Mary.

"And here I am now in me last days and filled with arthritis, diabetes and cancer and your right here by me side," said George.

Tears rolled down Mary's cheeks and she said, "Yes George, I'm here, I'm with you."

"Good Jasus Mary, you know, you've brought me nothing but bad luck," said George.

### When Old Friends Meet

Paddy and Mick met each other at the Belmont Tavern in St. John's after twenty years of not seeing each other. Following an exchange of greetings and amazement at running into each other after so many years, Paddy asked Mick, "How's the family doing?"

"Oh fine, fine," answered Mick. "We're a musical bunch for sure. I learned to play the accordion, the wife took up piano, young John plays the trumpet and Nancy is great on the violin. Why don't you drop up to the house for a visit some night and we'll entertain ye. By the way, Paddy, how's your family coming along?"

"We're all the finest kind. We got into the self-defense craze a few years ago. I got meself a black belt in Karate, the wife got a black belt in Judo and my two sons are taking Kung Fu. Why don't you and the family drop over to our place some night and we'll kick the shit out of ye," replied Paddy.

### Happily Married

Fred and George were childhood friends who went their own way after graduating from high school. Some years later, the two ran into each other on Water Street in downtown St. John's. Fred asked George, "Did you ever get married?"

"No, I'm still single," answered George.

"Well, you really should find yourself a wife, George, there's nothing like it," said Fred. "When I come home in the evening from work, the little woman is there at the door to meet me. She takes my coat and hangs it up. Then I sit in on the sofa, and she removes my shoes and replaces them with a comfortable pair of slippers. She passes me the *Telegram* to read then disappears into the kitchen to prepare supper. Boy oh Boy, George, what a life. In less than an hour she calls me into the kitchen and serves the most delicious meal you could imagine. When the meal is finished, she tells me to go back to the living room and watch the evening news while she washes the dishes. Then when the dishes and the kitchen are spic and span, she comes in and sits beside me on the sofa. She puts her arms around me and she talks. And she talks, and she talks, and she talks. Good Jesus George, I wish that woman would drop dead!"

### He's Drowning

Ned, Paddy and Bill, three inebriates from St. John's, spent a day in the woods on the Salmonier Line. Ned returned to the campfire from a visit down to the pond and said, "There's a fella down at the pond."

"What's he doing, swimming?" asked Paddy.

"No, he's not swimming," answered Ned as he put some boughs on the fire.

"Is he trouting?" asked Bill

"No, he's not trouting," replied Ned.

"Well what in hell's flames is he doing?" Bill asked.

"Drowning," answered Ned.

### Tommy Meets the Monsignor

Tommy Toe had raised enough money to buy a flask of rum for himself. He was walking west on Water Street when he met Monsignor Murphy from St. Patrick's Parish. The Monsignor politely commented, "How are you today, Tommy?"

Grasping the flask of rum a little tighter and placing it inside his famous old overcoat, he answered, "I only got enough for myself."

### Buck King

In his last years, Buck King lived in a house behind the softball diamond off Cabot Street. He was always there to participate in fun games and exhibition games during special events. I remember organizing several talent shows with Jen Adams at the CLB Armoury.

Bucky's neighbour Jim Lush would come to me complaining that I told Buck about the contest too early. He explained, "Buck is up all hours of the night practicing. We can't get any sleep."

One particular event was especially memorable. Dr. Paddy McNichols, Mrs. McNicholas, Ted Godden, Hugh Shea and Rita Dobbin comprised the panel of judges for the contest. There was an unwritten rule at these events that no matter how bad Buck sang, he would always be chosen the winner.

People were dressed up in nineteen-fifties' style for the occasion, and the program included Al Jolsen and Elvis Presley impersonators and a variety of other acts. Just as the contest started, members of a visiting motorcycle gang came into the hall.

Buck, wearing a ten gallon hat that almost covered his eyes, approached the microphone, strummed his guitar and began singing 'Who Took the Lock off the Hen House Door?' George McLaren of VOCM put his hands over his ears and his face showed pain. He asked me, "How long is Buck going to be singing?" Before I could answer, another problem arose.

While Buck struggled through his song, somebody, perhaps Jim Lush tossed a live hen onto the stage which startled Buck. Pandemonium broke out among the several acts off-stage waiting to go on. When Buck tried to run away from the squawking hen, his pants fell down.

Eventually, the hen was caught and removed from the hall, and Bucky managed to get his pants up again. The contest continued and the audience had a spirited laugh. However, when Buck King was announced winner of first prize, I was confronted by a huge biker shouting at me that the contest had to be fixed. "I never heard a worse singer in my life," he shouted. He had cornered me on the steps going to the stage and I gladly referred him to Hugh Shea at the Judges' Table. It took all Shea's talking skills to avoid a racket that night.

### Jen Adams Intervenes

Buck King was listening to a young contestant in a St. Paddy's Day talent show at the CLB Armory in St. John's sing, "Your Cheating Heart." He said to the person standing next to him, "That little boy is some singer!"

The person reacted indignantly, "That is not a boy, that is my daughter."

"I didn't know you were the father!" said Buck.

"I'm not, I'm her mother," said the woman.

Buck seemed confused when Jen Adams took him aside before he could continue with the conversation.

### Mascot for St. Pat's

Buck was about 4'2" and had an impish cherubic face. He was always a welcome site at Memorial Stadium during the hockey season. Buck wore a St. Pat's hockey shirt with C for Captain sewn on; a gift from the St. Pat's Hockey Team. During intermission, sometimes when tension ran high, Buck would skate onto the ice alone and handle the puck from one end of the rink to the other. The crowds chanted "go Buck go!" over and over until he slammed the puck into an open net. Then everyone in the stadium would come to their feet, whistling, clapping and cheering for Buck. He delighted in the fan reaction and grinned from ear to ear while waving his stick as he left the ice.

### Biggest Funeral

Buck passed away December 1990, and had one of the largest funerals ever seen in St. John's. The Basilica was filled to capacity. People from all walks of life turned out for the funeral. There were judges, lawyers, policemen, labourers, well-known sports figures, neighbourhood friends and politicians. Among them was Danny Williams who is reported to have commented to Judge Seabright, "Have you ever seen so many Dart's League jackets before?"

The affection for Buck King was evident among all classes of St. John's society.

### The Cappahayden Mule

In the early 1950s, a mule wandered along the shore and died in front of the Roman Catholic priests' residence at Cappahayden. The priest called the RCMP Office at Ferryland to report the incident with the expectation that they would arrange to remove the animal from the church property. The on-duty officer was a friend of the priest and the two often matched wits. When the priest told his friend of the dead mule, the officer asked, "Isn't it a priest's job to bury the dead?"

"Yes, but we have an obligation to contact the relatives first," replied the priest.

### Statue to Sir Richard Squires

Two fellows chatting on the tram "streetcar" going down Water Street:

Paddy: I'm in full support of putting a statue of Sir Richard Squires up in Bannerman Park.

Mick: For what?

Paddy: Well, it will give shade in the summer, shelter in winter and the birds a chance to speak for us all."

### Angus Wanted loan

Angus was a character of old St. John's who was in a constant battle with the demon liquor. Occasionally he would take the pledge to drink no more, and weeks later would lapse back into being a prisoner of the bottle. On this occasion, Angus went into the old Ritz Tavern on New Gower Street and asked Tommy, the bartender, for a loan of twenty dollars. He told Tommy, "Me mother-in-law died and I want to send her a wreath."

Tommy opened the cash and, after counting the money, said, "All I can come up with is

$17.75!"

"That's all right, Tommy," said Angus, "I'll take the $2.25 you're short in beer!"

### Angus and the Gosling Library

Angus decided he was going to join the library and take up reading as a hobby. He went to the old Gosling Library on Duckworth Street where he asked the Librarian for a good book to read.

"Do you want something light or heavy," asked the librarian.

"Doesn't matter," answered Angus, "I got my car with me."

## Stuff It

Angus was having an argument with a telephone operator at the Avalon Telephone Company in St. John's over questionable charges which had appeared on his bill. Finally, he became so angry that he told the operator, "Take the phone and shove it up your ass!"

"I don't have to listen to this. I'm going to have your phone taken out," replied the operator.

That afternoon, two men from the telephone company showed up at Angus' house to remove the telephone. Angus asked if he could make one call before the phone was removed and the man agreed.

Angus dialed a number and said, "Are you the lady I told to shove this phone up your ass?

"Yes, I am" said the lady.

"Well get ready, they're bringing the phone," said Angus.

## Angus Flies Air Canada

When Angus made his first airplane flight in 1952, he was so nervous he felt like throwing up. When he took his seat near the window on a Trans Canada Airlines flight to Halifax, a tall rugged-looking, but well-dressed man took the seat next to him. Angus quickly learned that his travelling companion was a college wrestler. Once in the air, the wrestler fell asleep and Angus felt even more nauseous. He was too timid to awake the giant beside him. He was unable to control his nausea and threw up all over the wrestler's blue serge suit. Fifteen minutes later, the wrestler awoke and was disturbed to see the mess all over his suit. Angus looked at him and said, "There now, do you feel better?"

## Hop Beer Stores and Shebeens

Angus was staggering down Water Street one night and bumped into a cop. Without making any apologies, he continued walking. The cop turned and said, "Hey fella! Do you know who I am?"

"Can't say I do, buddy," said Angus, "but if you'll tell me where you live, I'll help you home."

\* \* \*

Angus came out of a Hop Beer Shop on New Gower Street. He staggered a few hundred feet and seemed confused. He stopped a passerby and said, " Ehhh, pardon me sir, but where am I?"

"You're on the corner of Queen Street and New Gower Street," the man replied.

"Ahh! Cut out the details, what town am I in?" asked Angus.

\* \* \*

On another occasion, after spending an evening at a Hop Beer Shop, Angus was arrested on his way home to Cuddihy Street. The next morning, he appeared before Magistrate John Pius Mulcahey, who knew him well.

"Angus, Angus," said Mulcahey, "here you are again charged with habitual drunkenness. What's your explanation this time?"

"Habitual thirst, your honour," replied Angus.

"Angus, when are you going to stop drinking?" asked Mulcahey.

"When they stop making it," answered Angus.

\* \* \*

Angus was visiting a friend who passed him a bowl of grapes and invited him to take some. Angus pushed them aside and said, "I don't take my wine in pills."

## Sweet Shop

Angus was watching a woman struggling with a hot cup of tea at the Sweet Shop on Water Street. He took pity on her plight and approached her saying, "Here, you can have my tea. It's already saucered and blowed."

## Angus Laments

Angus said, "When I die, I want to go like my Uncle Joe who went in his sleep, not screaming like the other three people in his car."

\* \* \*

Angus, "The second day of a diet is much easier than the first. By the second day, I'm off it!"

### Black Shorts

Angus was among the first in town to go to a Water Street Strip Club. Next day, he told his wife that he was turned on by black underwear. After hearing this comment, his wife didn't wash his shorts for a month.

### The Present Incumbent

Joey Smallwood was campaigning in the Trinity District during the first general-election campaign after Confederation. He walked into a barn where an old gentleman was stacking hay for his horses and while shaking hands with the man said, "Mr. Smith, I am so sorry to learn of your wife's death."

"What did you say, sir?" asked Mr. Smith

"I said that I am very sorry to hear that your wife has recently died," replied Mr. Smallwood.

Displaying a puzzled look, Mr. Smith said, "I think there's some mistake bout dat, sir. I left de ole woman in good health this mawnin,' Mr. Smallwood. Who said she was dead?" asked Smith.

"Well, a few days ago, your pastor visited me in St. John's and told me the sad news," answered Smallwood.

The puzzling look on old Mr. Smith's face quickly disappeared and he commented, "Oh yes now I understan's quite well Mr. Smallwood. That was the former wife of mine. She died more den four weeks ago. The present incumbent is the finest kind b'y."

### Blackguard

When Joey Smallwood asked an opposition member, who was speaking in the Newfoundland Legislature to yield the floor to him, the member answered, " I never yield to blackguards."

As Smallwood sat back in his seat, he said, "I always do, Mr. Speaker!"

### Heckler

A fisherman, attending a political rally, was heckling the Liberal incumbent for Bonavista South, Ross Barbour, when the candidate warned him, "You don't seem to realize on which side your bread is buttered!"

"Doesn't make any difference," answered the fisherman, " I eat both sides!"

### In The House

The Honourable Gus Duffy, an opposition member of the Newfoundland Legislature, stood in the house to reply to a speech given by the Honourable William Keough. He began by saying, "Your speech was quite good, but there were some points beyond my reach."

The Honourable Greg Power interjected, "I once had a dog that had the same trouble with fleas."

### Electrifying

At a Legislative Committee investigating high electric costs, the representative for the Newfoundland Light and Power Company said, "Think of the good the Light and Power Company has done. If I were permitted a pun, I would say, 'Honour the Light Brigade.'"

Ank Murphy, MHA for St. John's Centre, quipped, "Oh what a charge they made!"

### Religion and Politics

The following story was told about Joey Smallwood during the 1950s and early 1960s and is no doubt from the same mythology that claims that Joey told the fishermen of Newfoundland to burn their boats. Yet, it is funny and part of our heritage of humour.

In a 1950s Newfoundland General election, at a time when religion played a major role in politics, Myles Murray was the Liberal candidate in the district of Ferryland. During a political rally in that predominantly Catholic district, Smallwood drew loud applause after telling the following story. He said that when he was a boy growing up in the west end of St. John's, he would get up early Sunday morning, hitch the horse to its carriage and drive his Catholic grandparents to St. Patrick's Church on Patrick Street where he would accompany them to mass then drive them home. Later in the morning, he took the carriage to the home of his Protestant grandparents and drove them to the Wesley United Church on Patrick Street where he would attend service with them and drive them home afterwards. Smallwood concluded his remarks by saying, "Because of my background, I have always had a great respect for Catholics and Protestants."

On the drive back to St. John's, Myles Murray complimented him on his speech and on how well it had been received. He added, "But Joe, I didn't know that you had Catholic grandparents."

"Well, to tell you the truth Myles, we didn't even have a horse," explained Smallwood.

## Joey and Billy Brown

During debate in the Newfoundland Legislature, Billy Brown, the member for St. John's west, was criticizing Smallwood for building the Premier's residence so far from St. John's at Roache's Line. After describing the size of the property, he noted, "On a drive there recently, coming up Roache's Line, I could see the large wooden horse that used to be in front of a Water Street Store years ago. The Premier now has it placed on top of a hill where it can be seen for miles. I noticed that its rear end was facing the road."

At this point, Smallwood quipped, "Perhaps the horse saw who was coming."

Adelaide St.

Boys from Flower Hill.

Coal delivery.

*All photos courtesy of City of St. John's Archives*
Kenny's Fruit Store, corner of New Gower St. and Brazil Sq.

# Chapter 4

# Wit and Humour
# from the 1890s and 1930s

During the period from the 1890's to the 1930's, there was a particular interest shown in humour by Newfoundland's many newspapers. Most newspapers featured humour columns, often obtained from England, Ireland and Scotland. Stories from these columns found their way into local wit and humour. This may have sparked some of the humour introduced in local news coverage, particularly court news, which was popular among readers. The *Evening Telegram* court news, for a period after 1907, was called *Meeting out Justice in Judge Flannery's Court*. Judge Flannery lived on Prescott Street and was a neighbour of Johnny Burke. Humour was displayed on a daily basis in Flannery's Court, and the feature's anonymous reporter added his own witty interpretation to his coverage. In addition, there were many newspaper bloopers found in the reporting of legitimate news and countless stories of local characters who were always a source of old time humour. This chapter has drawn upon these sources for your enjoyment.

## During Spanish Flu Epidemic – 1918

During the height of the flu epidemic of 1918, an Upper Island Cove couple, George and Bessey, came to St. John's to visit a relative at the old General Hospital on Forest Road. Precautions were being taken all over the city, and the Department of Health had a variety of warning signs placed in the corridors of the hospitals. While waiting for the elevator, George noticed a sign on the wall which read, "Spitting Prohibited – You could be fined $5.00." Inside the elevator, Bessey said, "George, I'm feeling stomach sick."

"Not here Bessey, for Gawd's sake! It costs five dollars just to spit," said George.

## Playful Dog

"Have you seen Papa's new dog Rover," asked Betsy.

"Yes," Jimmy replied uneasily. "I have had the pleasure of meeting the dog."

"Isn't he splendid? He is so affectionate," said Betsy.

"Yes, I noticed he was very demonstrative," said Jimmy as he moved uneasily in his chair.

"He is very playful, too. I never saw a more playful animal in all my life," said Betsy.

"You're not going to let him in this room tonight, are you?" asked Jimmy.

"Why?" Betsy enquired.

"Because I was a little afraid that when he bit that piece out of me the other evening, he was in earnest. But if it was only in play, of course it's all right. I can take fun as well as anybody," answered Jimmy.

## An Intended Good Deed!

In the early hours of the morning, a man passing the Atlantic Hotel on Duckworth Street in old St. John's noticed a man leaning limply against the front entrance. "What's wrong?" he asked. "Drunk?"

"Yup."

"Do you stay at this hotel?

"Yup."

"Do you want me to help you in?"

"Yup."

With much difficulty, he half-dragged, half-carried the drooping figure up the stairway to the second floor. "What floor do you live on?" he asked. "Is this it?"

"Yup."

Rather than face a possible angry wife who might, perhaps, take him for a companion more at fault than her spouse, he opened the nearby door and pushed the man into the darkened room.

The good Samaritan made his way downstairs, and as he exited the building, he saw the figure of a second man, apparently in worse condition than the first one.

"What's the matter," he asked. "Are you drunk, too?"

"Yup."

"Are you staying at this hotel?"

"Yup."

"Do you need help upstairs?"

"Yup."

The good Samaritan pushed, pulled and carried him to the second floor, where this man said he was staying. He opened the same door and pushed the man inside.

Once more, as he left the hotel, he saw a third man who appeared to be in worse shape than the other two. He was about to approach the man and offer help when the man lurched out into the street and grabbed the arm of a passing policeman. "Offshur! Offshur! Fer heaven's sake, Offshur," he said, "save me from that man. He's done nothin' all night long but carry me upstairs and throw me down the elevator shaft."

The Atlantic Hotel was one of only a few buildings in the St. John's of the 1890s that had an elevator.

### Fella from Fortune

A fellow from Fortune got a job with the Newfoundland Railway. On his first trip across the Island, he forgot the name of the station where the train had just arrived, so he shouted into the car, "Here ye are for where ye are going. All in there for here, come out!"

## Who Needs Whitewashing

During 1895, Sir Robert Bond was involved in political controversy over Newfoundland's financial situation. Some felt he 'whitewashed' many of government's short-comings. This prompted the *Daily News* to print, as a news item, the following item. Its headline read:

### Ah Jon Sing Kicks

*Ah Jon Sing wants a monopoly of the whitewash business and resents the intrusion of Fong-Joo and Soo-oo-Hin.*

*He claims that the government are not so much in need of the cleansing properties of soap and water as they are of the virtues of whitewash. It is not cleaning off but glossing over that is desired by them.*

*Ah Jon Sing has another cause of complaint. "The wealth of Ormus, of Ind and of far Cathay," was to reach us by the railway, at least so Mr. Bond has declared. Our celestial visitors reached us by the Polina. Ah Jon Sing is therefore indignant and justly so. He has shown his ability as a whitewasher and now he demands the monopoly. He deserves it and is right in kicking.*

– **Daily News, August 21, 1895**

## Misunderstood

During World War I, several hundred soldiers of the Newfoundland Regiment were stationed over in England. One of them was a Jimmy Chafe from Kilbride. One day his father Bill received a telegram from young Jimmy which stated, "Send seven pounds." Bill Chafe had killed a cow just the day before he received the telegram, and not knowing anything about the pounds, shillings and pence currency of England, thought that Jimmy had somehow gotten word of the killing of the cow, and was now asking for seven pounds of it!

## Clerical Wit

An occasional humour column that appeared in the *Evening Telegram* between 1915 and 1920 was entitled "Clerical Wit" which originated in Ireland and was well received in Newfoundland. It is included in this collection as an example of the type of humour Newfoundlanders enjoyed in Colonial times. The following sample was taken from these columns:

*Most clergymen are not at all lacking in a sense of humour. There was, for instance, Nicholas Burke, better known as Father Thomas Burke, the great Irish patriot and preacher. Father Tom had a great fondness for riding on the top of an omnibus. Once when doing so after a long church service in Dublin, he produced his breviary (special-prayer-book) and was soon deep in its contents. A well-known evangelical sitting nearby took upon himself to comment upon the act. "The Lord tells us," he said, "'that when we pray, we should not be as the hypocrites, who love to pray in public and at the corners of streets that they may be seen by men. Now, when I pray, I enter into my closet, and when I have shut the door, I pray in secret.'"*

*Without looking up, Father Burke replied aloud, "Yes, and then you get on the top of an omnibus and tell everyone all about it."*

## Razor Back

In November 1916, a farmer at Witless Bay claimed damages against the Reid Newfoundland Company because its number nine train frightened his pig and caused it to charge and destroy a fence on his property. The pig died from injuries sustained in the mishap. His claim was written in poetic form as follows:

### The Pig 'n' Railway

*Dear Sir:*
*My razor back went on your track*

*one week ago today,*
*when number nine came down the line*
*and snuffed his life away.*
*Now razor back through no fault of mine*
*broke down my garden gate.*
*So please, sir, pen a cheque for ten*
*this claim to liquidate.*

C.W. Chard, Claims Agent for Reid Newfoundland, handled the claim and was up to the occasion. His reply to Tobin read:

*If your razor back went on our track*
*sure everybody knows*
*that razor backs on railway tracks*
*are bound to meet their woes.*
*No swine kind was on our mind*
*the day we laid the track.*
*The branch was built for number nine*
*and not for razor back.*
— *Sincerely, C.W. Chard*

## Old Cemetery Epitaphs

For Sammy Maher
Please shed a tear,
He cranked his car
While still in gear.

And give a sigh
for Howard Oake
He didn't know
His brakes were broke.

## Pennies from Heaven

A rabbi, a Catholic priest, and an Anglican minister were discussing how they divided their church collections each week between the poor of their parish, which was God's share, and themselves.

"I draw a square on the ground, toss the money into the air and what lands in the square is mine. The rest is God's share," explained the priest.

The minister said, "Well, I draw a circle on the ground, toss the money in the air and what lands in the circle I keep, the rest goes for the poor."

The rabbi said, "I simply throw all the money in the air and what God wants for the poor, he keeps. Whatever he allows to fall to the ground, I keep."

### The Blockhouse

The Blockhouse was a landmark on top of Signal Hill long before Cabot Tower was built. The Blockhouse was destroyed by fire on April 28, 1894. Cabot Tower replaced it and was formally opened on June 20, 1900. In the early part of the twentieth century, a man named Johnnie Power was blown to bits when the noon day gun exploded near the Cabot Tower on Signal Hill. Power was buried at Mount Carmel Cemetery by the undertaker Jimmy Martin. Some saw humour in the tragedy as demonstrated by a surviving epitaph penned at the time of the accident.

> Here lies the body of John Power
> Who played with the gun at Cabot Tower
> The gun went off and shook the nation
> And they found John Power at the Railway station.

### The Blue Puttee Parrot

A big attraction at "The Blue Puttee Restaurant and Hall," which originally operated at the corner of King's Road and Gower Street and later moved to Rawlin's Cross, St. John's, was an old parrot named Benny who had a large vocabulary and greeted customers as they arrived and departed from the establishment. One day, a middle-aged gentleman named Sandy visited the restaurant for the first time. When Benny saw him, he began flapping his wings and pacing back and forth in his cage shouting, "You're the ugliest man I have ever seen. Look at that big nose, and those big ears. There's more wrinkles in your face than in a crinkle. Boy! You are the ugliest."

The manager, who was embarrassed by Benny's outrageous display rushed over, and as he shook the cage, told Benny to keep quiet or he would lock him in the basement for a month. Benny settled down on his perch, but his eyes remained focused on Sandy.

Sandy was terribly upset by the incident. He sat alone, and after finishing his lunch got up to pay the bill. He realized that he still had to pass the parrot on the way out. Sandy wondered if the parrot would make another terrible scene. After paying the bill, he made his way towards the front door. Benny's eyes were still focused on him. When Sandy passed in front of the cage, Benny leaned forward and in a low voice loud enough for Sandy to hear drawled, "You kno-o-o-w!"

## The *Daily News* Subscription

Newspapers frequently receive curious letters from their readers, but the following received at the *Daily News* in St. John's in 1908 stands out as a real gem.

> *Dear Sir,*
>
> *When I subscribed to the* Daily News *a year ago, you stated that if I was not satisfied at the end of the year, I could have my money back. Well, I would like to have it back. On second thought, to save you the trouble, you may apply it to my next year's subscription!"*
>
> *– R. H, at Portugal Cove South*

## "On The List"

In 1907, the police attempted to reduce the number of drunks being brought into court each day on various charges stemming from intoxication by circulating what became known as "The Drunk List" among the liquor outlets throughout St. John's. All those who appeared in court on liquor related charges were placed on the list, and a copy was given to each liquor store. In response, Jimmy Murphy, who was a partner in writing with Johnny Burke, penned the song called "On The List."

> Oh! Danny, dear, I heard the "cops"
> On Yesterday they dropped
> A notice to all rum-shops
> For to say our drinks are stopped
> I'm told, my wife, and yours also,
> To do so, did insist,
> We dare not to the "gin mill" go,
> For now we're on the list.
>
> Chorus
> No more the police shall "run us in,"
> With a bracelet on each wrist.
> We're done of "loading to the chin,"
> For now we're on the list.
>
> No more we'll stagger home at night,
> To kick and cuff and swear,
> Our little children from our sight,
> And to tear our poor wife's hair.
> The "pleasures" that they did endure,
> They never will be missed,
> Oh! Danny, dear, they have found the cure"
> For now, we're on the list.
>
> Oh! Danny, dear, I do declare,
> "Tis the best thing that could be,
> To keep us from going "on the beer,"
> For "twould ruin both you and me.
> Too long unto the gin-mill, Dan,
> We brought our hard-earned grist,
> So, cheer up, Dan, shake hands, 'old man,"
> For now, we're on the list.

### Desperate for Rum

In 1918, a man trying to raise the price of "a drink of the national" stole his wife's boots and tried to sell them. He was caught by a police officer on patrol and the next day the incident was reported in the *Evening Telegram* as follows:

### Selling Wife's Boots

*Saturday afternoon Sergeant Mackey discovered an outport man buying a pair of woman's boots from a resident of the city. Knowing that the man was a hard drinker, he discovered that he was selling the boots for a couple of shillings to buy drink. Sergeant Mackey took the boots and restored them to the unfortunate wife and sent the seller and would-be purchaser about their business.*

### Dickey Pittman

Dickey Pittman was standing at the bar in Casey's Tavern on Duckworth Street, St. John's. He told the bartender, "I was in the woods last weekend with me buddies and I came face to face with a bear. I took me rifle and fired, and I hit him right between the 'Yours.'"

"What's yours?" asked the bartender.

"Whiskey, with ginger ale," replied Dickey.

### McGuire's Dandykake

During the late summer of 1915, McGuire's Bakery in St. John's conducted a special promotion for their popular product, "Dandykake." Two hundred and fifty dollars in cash prizes were offered to introduce "Dandykake" to the market. The advertisement in the *Evening Telegram* of September 7, 1915, explained, "A tag will be placed in a loaf of McGuire's Bread each week, and the lucky person who presents that tag at McGuire's Bakery will be given ten dollars, and to the proprietor of the store where the loaf was purchased, five dollars will be given."

This ad was followed on September 10, 1915, with the "McGuire's Dandykake" song:

*Oh, wifey dear, and did you hear, the news that's on the go,*
*McGuire's Bread contains a tag, ten dollars worth you know.*
*The one who strikes the lucky loaf,*
*They'll jump with joy "my boys,"*
*And "heel it" to McGuire's, to get the promised prize.*

*McGuire's Bread "it can't be beat," it's worth its weight in gold,*
*In every home in St. John's, it is prized by young and old.*
*And now, there is his Dandykake, a dandy 'tis no doubt,*
*It will melt, with sugar icing, just like butter in your mouth.*

*So wifey buy McGuire's loaf, good weight I do declare,*
*Maybe a tag in one of them, we may locate my dear.*
*If I were you, I would eschew, your homemade bread to bake,*
*Until we find a prize-tag, in McGuire's Dandykake.*

McGuire's Bakery was famous for its "O'Boy Bread" and was located on Adelaide Street north of New Gower Street.

### Genuine News Items!

The following two items appeared, as presented, in the St. John's *Evening Telegram*, April 4, 1910. The first item describes how young boys harassed a funeral procession:

### Disgraceful Conduct

Some young fellows of the East End behaved disgracefully yesterday by chasing a pig while the funeral procession of the late Ernest Snow was going to the cemetery at Forest Road. They drove the pig through the funeral ranks several times, and continued 'til some gentlemen stopped them.

### Too Well Known

A married woman, whose husband has often been in court, was on a passenger ship leaving St. John's on Saturday afternoon when her better-half reported to Superintendent

*Grimes that the woman was taking all his clothes away with her. He asked that the police stop the ship so that he could get his clothes and secure a divorce, after which the woman could go "to Jericho if she pleased."* He became so insolent that he narrowly escaped being run into the cells, and was unceremoniously ejected from the lock-up.

### The Hen and the Dog

Parsons: "Sorry old timer that my hen got loose and tore up your flowers."

Murphy: "That's all right, cause my dog ate your hen!"

Parsons: "Good, I just ran over your dog and killed him!"

### What's Radio?

Shortly after radio was introduced in Newfoundland, Bessie Carney of Casey Street asked her nephew John to explain for her what a radio was. John gave the question some thought, then explained, "Aunt Bessie, if you had a really long dog that stretched from St. John's to Carbonear and you stepped on its tail in St. John's, it would bark in Carbonear. Now that would be telegraphy. But radio is exactly the same only without the dog."

### We Need Bread!

Mrs. Murphy went to the Court House in St. John's and pleaded with Judge Nugent to let her husband out of the lock-up.

"What's he in for?" asked the Judge.

"He stole a loaf of bread," said Mrs. Murphy.

"Is he a decent father?" asked the Judge.

"No, your honour. He's rotten. He drinks, hits the kids and gambles."

"Well, why do you want him back?" asked the Judge.

"We're out of bread again," answered Mrs. Murphy.

## Lucy Left Leg

The operator of a boarding house on Tank Lane (Cuddihy Street near Barter's Hill) was a lady who became well-known to the courts due to circumstances often involving her boarders. She was nick-named Lucy Left Leg because when drinking alcohol, her right leg would give out, leaving her to limp around on her left leg. Her husband, whom we shall refer to as Charlie, was a henpecked man who would not dare question his wife unless he had a few drops of the *National* in him.

### Lucy Left Leg and the Boarder

Lucy Left Leg took one of her boarders to court whom she claimed had not paid his board for three months. She told Judge Knight that Paddy, the boarder, was supposed to pay thirty-dollars a month board and now owed her ninety dollars, which she was claiming. Thirty dollars a month was well above boarding rates in St. John's in the early twentieth century. Judge Knight was skeptical of her claim and put her through her paces while questioning her. Paddy was known to have a reasonably good income, but liked a drink, and the Judge suspected Lucy Left Leg had taken advantage of him.

"How much a month were you charging?" Judge Knight asked.

"Thirty dollars!" answered Lucy Left Leg.

"That's thirty dollars per month?" the Judge asked.

"Yes, thirty dollars a month!" replied Lucy Left Leg.

"That's thirty dollars a month, each month for three months?" asked Judge Knight.

"Yes, for three months!" the impatient Lucy answered.

"That's a total of ninety dollars!" stated Judge Knight.

"My gawd, yer Honour, yes, it's ninety dollars," answered Lucy Left Leg who was obviously irritated by the judges drawing out of the questioning.

"Now, Lucy, you want me to believe that your boarding house on Cuddihy Street is worth thirty dollars a month?" asked Judge Knight.

"It certainly is!" snapped Lucy Left Leg.

"Now Lucy, answer me with either 'yes' or 'no'. If I were to go to your house and ask to be taken in as a boarder, would you have the gall to charge me thirty dollars monthly?" asked Judge Knight.

"Well, no."

Judge Knight interrupted before she could finish and said, "See, I told you! I told you!"

"You wouldn't give me a chance to finish. I was telling you no, I would make YOU pay six months board up front!" Lucy Left Leg shot back.

Judge Knight wasn't impressed and decided in the boarder's favour.

### Lucy Left Leg's Charity

Allen Kirby went to the door of Lucy Left Leg's Boarding House on Cuddihy Street and asked Lucy, "How about giving me something to eat, I'm really hungry?"

"Would you like some of yesterday's leftovers?" asked Lucy.

"I'd love it," said Allen.

"Good. Come back tomorrow," said Lucy, as she slammed the door in his face.

### Lucy Argues with Spouse

Lucy Left Leg's husband Charlie staggered home late one night after drinking hop beer all day. Lucy refused to let him in the house. Charlie shouted, "Hey Lucy, if you don't open the door and let me in, I'm gonna tell everybody I slept with you before we were married!"

"Go ahead, and I'll tell them you weren't the first one!" Lucy shouted back.

Charlie reminded Lucy, "You never had a rag to put on your back before you married me!"

Lucy answered, "Well, I got plenty of them now!"

### Lucy Left Leg's Best!

Tomcat Neill was having lunch at Lucy Left Leg's boarding house on Cuddihy Street. He had just started eating when Lucy bragged, "You're getting a good meal there, Tomcat. The two things I make best are a good Irish Stew and a blueberry pie!"

"Well, which one is this?" asked Tomcat, as he forked into his food.

### Lucy Left Leg at the Dentist

Lucy Left Leg only went to the dentist when she wanted to get a tooth removed. She always found something to complain about, and the dentist didn't look forward to her visits.

"How much are ya going to pick my pocket today to take out one tooth?" Lucy Left Leg asked.

"Five dollars," answered the dentist.

"Five dollars for a minutes work! I should charge ya with robbery," commented Lucy Left Leg.

"Now Lucy, if it will make you feel better, I can extract the tooth very, very slowly," said the dentist in a deliberately calm voice.

When it was all over, the dentist said, "There now, no swelling. You have the face of a Saint."

Then under his breath he whispered, "A Saint Bernard!"

### Christmas at Lucy Left Leg's

On Christmas Day 1930, Paddy Murphy was making the rounds of his neighborhood wishing all a Merry Christmas. He walked into the kitchen of Lucy Left Leg, and noticing a sprig of mistletoe over the kitchen doorway, said to Lucy, "Would ya give me a kiss under the mistletoe?"

"Paddy, I wouldn't kiss you under chloroform!" Lucy replied.

### The Russian Boarder

Lucy Left Leg went into the Newfoundland Saving's Bank to deposit fifty-thousand rubles her Russian boarder had given her before he departed on the *Fort Amherst* that morning for New York City. Lucy had given him room and board in her house for six weeks, and was delighted when he offered her fifty-thousand rubles for her hospitality. When the clerk calculated the value of

Lucy's rubles into Canadian money, she told Lucy, "Fifty-thousand rubles are worth fifty-seven cents in Canadian money."

"Fifty-seven cents for six weeks board. That son-of-a-bitch," said Lucy. "I even packed a lunch for him to take on the boat."

### Went Out

Allen Kirby told his friend Paddy Murphy that Lucy and Charlie were married twenty years, and the only time they went out together was when the gas stove in the kitchen exploded.

### Lucy Shopping

Lucy went into Ayre & Sons on Water Street to buy a shirt for her husband Charlie. "What size shirt do your husband take?" asked the clerk.

"I don't know," said Lucy, "but if it's any help, I can just get my two hands around his neck."

### Fat Back for Brains

Lucy was known to say, "If brains were fat back, poor Charlie wouldn't have enough to fry a touton!"

### Dirty Windows

When Lucy Left Leg saved enough money to have her house professionally cleaned, the cleaners removed so much dirt that they found two windows she didn't know she had.

### Board Up to Date

Paddy Murphy called at Lucy Left Leg's for his friend Salt Water Bill. As the two walked down Tank Lane, Paddy said, "I see you must have paid Lucy your board arrears."

"What makes ya think that?" asked Salt Water.

"Well, when I went into the kitchen you were eating chicken breast. If you were behind in board, you'd be lucky if Lucy let you have the wing," answered Paddy.

## Brave O'Rielley

O'Rielley had been cheating on his Missus for years. His poor wife found out and confronted him. The years had hardened O'Rielley and he was bold enough to answer, "So what!" He wasn't satisfied to leave it at that and he added, "In fact, I have a date tonight! And who do you think is going to get my suit pressed and ready for my date? You are! And who do you think is going to shine my shoes? You are! And do you know who's going to tie my tie?"

"Yes," said Mrs. O'Rielley, "the undertaker!"

Paddy Murphy asked the bartender at Casey's, "Can you give me a beer on tick (credit)?"

The bartender replied, "I be terribly sorry, old fella, but my tick beer is so thick that you couldn't drink it. In fact, it's too thick to pour. Now I have some "pay-money beer" that's just as good and ya can have one for ten cents."

## St. John's Auctioneer

In the 1920s, a St. John's auctioneer was auctioning off a bust which was part of items collected from an elegant old home in the east end of St. John's.

"What am I offered for this absolutely beautiful bust of Plato?" he asked.

"That's not Plato," interrupted a refined gentleman in the crowd, "that's Aristotle."

"Sorry folks," explained the auctioneer, "the jokes on me. It only goes to show how much I know about the Bible."

## The Wit at St. Barb

This story took place at Parsons Pond in the 1920's, where the search for oil was very active a hundred years ago. On this occasion, an Englishman arrived at Parsons Pond, and while out for a walk, met a man named Azariah who was one of the older residents of the community. After exchanging the customary pleasantries, the Englishman asked, "Have you a telegraph office here?"

"No, we have no telegraph office," answered Azariah.

"Perhaps you have a wireless office then?" asked the visitor.

"No, no wireless office," responded Azariah.

"Well, have you any radios?" asked the Englishman.

"No, not a radio in the place. There was one, but it's not working," said Azariah.

"My Gawd," said the Englishman in amazement, "No telegraph office! No wireless! No radios! I expect you people here don't hear very much of what goes on in London, do you?"

"No, we don't, but then over in London I don't suppose they hear much news of what goes on here either," answered Azariah.

### The Tsunami

In the aftermath of the 1929 Tidal Wave in Newfoundland, a reporter asked an old fellow named Ned what he was thinking when the tidal wave rushed into the harbour at Burin and over land, flooding and destroying everything ahead of it?

"What was I thinking, ya ask? With the roar of the water and the sound of buildings and boats being crushed and people screaming, what man with the use of his two legs to run with, and his lungs to roar with, would be after thinkin' at all at a time like that?"

### Crossing the River

In the early 1920's, a St. John's merchant was taking his family for a drive along Conception Bay in his new automobile. He came to a river crossing and was about to turn back when he noticed a farmer looking over a nearby fence. The merchant asked the farmer if it was safe to drive his car across the river.

"Shouldn't be any problem at all, sir," answered the farmer.

The man told his family they were going to cross the river and go on for a few more miles to take in the beautiful scenery. He drove only a short distance when the water came up over the car and almost into the windows. The angry merchant shouted to the farmer and demanded an explanation as to why he said the river was safe when it wasn't.

"I can't understand it at all," said the farmer, "the water only comes up halfway on our ducks."

### Plenty of Catsup

Moses Hamilton returned to his home-town in Fortune Bay having lived in Boston for more than ten years. After getting settled away in the old family home, he dropped down to the merchant's store to visit his old friend Tom. As he entered the store, he noticed that the front windows were filled with bottles of catsup. Inside the store, Moses noted that all the shelves also displayed catsup. Tom was happy to see his old friend and came out from behind the counter to welcome him. Moses said, "Jasus, Tom, I've never seen so much catsup."

"Think so, Moses," said Tom, "well, follow me." Tom took Moses to the cellar below which was blocked with boxes of catsup.

"Cods heads!" exclaimed Moses. "You must sell a lot of catsup!"

"Not at all," replied Tom, "I buy it from a salesman who comes here every month, and boy, can he ever sell catsup!"

### The Blanket

Paddy was traveling to Port aux Basques in a sleeping car on the Newfoundland Express. The woman in the upper berth shouted to him, "Hey, mister, it's getting really cold, could you get me another blanket?"

Paddy answered, "It is kinda cold, how about pretending we're married?"

After a brief silence, the woman replied, "Well, all right."

"In that case, get your own gawdam blanket!" said Paddy.

### Broken Flask

A well-known story around St. John's, sometimes told today, had its origins in the 1920s. It is supposed to be a true story. There was an old fellow in St. John's who dearly loved a drink of Demerara Rum. This was in the days when "flasks" were all many people could afford. Scraping up enough money one day to buy a flask, he hurried to the liquor store and made his purchase. It was in winter and the streets were extremely slippery. Hurrying out of the store with the flask in his hip pocket, he forgot about the slippery condition of the streets in his eagerness to get at the flask of rum as quickly as possible. He was no sooner outside then, plunk! His feet went out from under him and he fell flat on his arse. He didn't mind that, but when he stood up, he felt something trickling down his leg. "Gosh," he whispered, fearing to believe the worst, "I hope 'tis blood."

### The Governor's Maid

During the 1930s in St. John's, there was a cab driver named John Stamp who did a lot of cab work for Government departments. He often parked in front of the railway station on Water Street West to pick up arriving passengers destined for the General Hospital. One day he was asked to go to the station to pick up a new housemaid who was arriving by train to work at Government House. Mr. Stamp asked the conductor if he knew of a girl who was coming to town to work for the Governor. The conductor pointed out the girl to him.

The cab driver approached the girl and asked if she had any valises or parcels. He gathered her luggage and told her to follow him. He noticed as they left the car and walked down the platform towards the station building that she was looking strangely at him. The look became more suspicious as they walked through the station building toward the taxi outside. Mr. Stamp was puzzled as to why the girl appeared to be so concerned.

Finally, he asked, "You're the girl for the Governor, aren't you?"

"I am," she answered.

As Mr. Stamp put her luggage into the trunk of his cab, she spoke up, "I don't believe you're the Governor at all!"

### Children's Song

The following item was a popular children's verse in the 1920s in and around St. John's.

*Daddy's get'n big and fat*
*The rest of us are thinner*
*'Cause the nickles go for beer*
*To wash down daddy's dinner.*

The verse was usually repeated during the children's game known as "Skipping." It would start off very slowly, and would be spoken faster and faster as the skipping pace increased.

### Old time popular parody
"I kissed her lips, and left her behind to you."

### Politician Gets Carried Away
In the days of Responsible Government, a famous old politician, while visiting the penitentiary on Forest Road, was called upon to give a speech to the prisoners. He was unprepared, fumbled around and then got a little carried away with his impromptu speech. He told the gathering:

> *I can't call you gentlemen, because no gentleman would be here. I can't call you fellow-citizens, as you lost your citizenship when you came here. I can't call you friends, because I would be giving myself away. All I can say is, inmates of the prison, I'm glad to see you here – glad to see so many of you here – wish there were more of you here. I understand you were elected unanimously to come here. I hope you will serve the colony faithfully. I know your seats will never be contested, and when you return to your constituents, I hope they will reseat you. I thank you."*

### The Doctor's Advice
Poor old Bessie had no idea that her daughter Joan was displaying all the signs of being pregnant. She took her to Doctor Tolson Smith on Long's Hill. It didn't take Dr. Smith long to determine that Joan was pregnant. His problem was how to break the news to the pious and innocent Bessie.

He thought he found a way when he asked, "Tell me, Bessie, has Joan ever had intercourse?"

Bessie hesitated in thought for a moment, then answered, "I don't know what you mean by intercourse, Doctor, but you can give it to her anyway. The welfare are paying for this."

### St. John's Council Replied in Verse

Before Confederation, a city homeowner applied to the St. John's City Council for a permit to repair his house. A man named John L. Slattery was secretary-treasurer of the Council at the time and sent the following reply, advising the man his request for a permit had been approved. The letter read:

> *Dear Sir:*
> *Your letter's contents duly noted,*
> *Request therein discussed and voted,*
> *And granted you have been given permission*
> *To proceed with every expedition,*
> *To start your architectural stunt,*
> *And burnish up your house's front,*
> *For after nineteen toilsome years,*
> *The house indeed must need repairs.*
> *I answer without fear of flattery,*
> *– Secretary-Treasurer John L. Slattery*

### The Wit of Sir Richard Squires

During his career as Prime Minister of Newfoundland, Sir Richard Squires came under a verbal attack in the Legislature. An opposition member was recounting the record of the Prime Minister. He emphasized the mistakes made and played down the achievements. In mentioning a few good things the Squires Administration had done, the speaker went on to take credit from Squires for those good things, and attributed the credit to himself. He then said that Squires had stolen those ideas from him. "Yes," he declared, "that's what you've done! You stole my ideas! You robbed my brains!"

At this point, Squires stood up and said:

"Mr. Speaker, in my public career in Newfoundland I have been charged with many things, accused of many crimes. As a rule, I do not bother to reply to these charges, but to the accusation which the honourable gentleman has just made, I must make a reply. The honourable gentleman says I have robbed his brains. This, sir, is the first time I have ever been charged with petty larceny!"

### The Fortune Harbour Merchant

The merchant at Fortune Harbour asked his son Tommy, "Did you put the water in the milk this morning?"

"I certainly did, dad," answered Tommy.

"Flaming squid heads, Tommy, don't you know that's wrong?" roared the merchant.

"B-b-b-but, dad, you told me to mix water in with the milk," explained Tommy.

"You never listen, do ya?" said the merchant. "I told you to pour the water in first and pour the milk into it. Then, we can tell our customers that we never, ever put water in our milk."

### Newspaper Bloopers

A man was killed in 1944 after being run over by a streetcar (tram) at the intersection of Leslie Street and Water Street in St. John's. The report which appeared in the *Daily News* the next day read, "The accident took place at the intersection of Leslie Street and Water Street as the dead man was crossing the intersection."

Another accident report around the same year stated, "The man was taken to St. Clare's Hospital for treatment, but left there this morning with no bones broken."

### Old Time Lighter Side! – 1915

Judge E. McCarthy: "You have plenty of impudence, Flannigan, to steal my chickens and then try to sell them to me."

The accused – Knobby Flannigan: "Why, yer honour, I thought you'd pay a better price for fowls you'd reared yourself. You know what yer buying then."

\* \* \*

When twins came their father, Paddy Dunn,
Gave "Edward" as a name to each son.
When folks said, "Absurd!"
He replied, "Ain't you heard,
That two Eds are better than one?"

\* \* \*

A young wife recently went into a butcher shop on Duckworth Street and addressed the butcher thus, "I bought three or four hams here a month or so ago and they were fine. Have you any more of them?"

"Yes, ma'am," replied the butcher, "there are ten of those hams hanging up there now."

"Well, if you're sure they're off the same pig, I'll take three of them," replied the young wife, meekly.

\* \* \*

On New Year's Eve 1915, two outport men were carried to the General Hospital in St. John's, victims of an explosion on their boat in the harbour. One had the misfortune to have his nasal organ blown off. The other had lost one of his ears.

The two were placed in adjacent beds, and in the morning, the one minus his nose shouted to his neighbour, "Happy New Year to ya, mate!"

"Happy new nose to ya-self, and mind yer own business," growled the other.

\* \* \*

Bessie O'Brien: Haven't you forgotten I gave you a piece of pie only yesterday?

George Snooks: Yes, ma'm, I've tried to forget and forgive.

\* \* \*

Parson: Young man, do you know how to dance?
Young Man: Well, I know the holds, but I don't know the steps.

\* \* \*

Grandfather Murphy lived to be ninety-five years old and never used glasses.

Nothing special about that, lots of people prefer to drink from a bottle.

### Fellow from Portugal Cove South

Din Hartery from Portugal Cove South went on board a schooner in St. John's Harbour and asked the captain for a job. The Captain, thinking he could have some fun at Din's expense said, "Certainly, if you can find four ends to this piece of rope." He handed a single piece of rope to Din.

"Four ends you say, Captain," muttered Din. He held up one end of the rope and said, "Here's one end."

"You're right," said the Captain.

Din then took the other end of the rope and showed the captain, "Here's another end, which makes two ends."

"Right again, Din," said the Captain.

"Well one end and two ends make three ends, Captain," said Din.

The Captain laughed and said, "But I asked for four ends."

Din said, "Yes, that you did." He then took the rope and tossed it into the harbour. "There's an end to the entire rope, Captain, and three ends and one more end makes four ends!"

Din Hartery got the job.

### Desperate Move

In the 1930s, a Harbour Grace man, well-known for his love of liquor, was told by his doctor, "Your drinking days are over. Just one more shot of rum and you are a dead man."

"Well, what will I do when I get edgy and want to calm my nerves?" the man asked.

"Have something to eat," replied the Doctor.

The man left the doctor's office after swearing he would never taste alcohol again. He was doing well for a couple of weeks. Then one night when walking along Harvey Street, he glanced into a window and saw a man hanging himself. He began to shake, then ran into a nearby restaurant and shouted, "Quick! Give me a potted meat sandwich!"

### Fighting Satan

During World War I, Doc Neil, one of the characters of old St. John's in the early nineteenth century, boarded the Newfoundland Express for a trip to visit relatives around the bay. A Salvation Army officer sat alongside him. The Doc sized up the officer's uniform and then asked, "What regiment do you belong to?"

The officer answered, "I am a soldier of the Lord. I am going to Clarenville to battle the devil, then to Gander to fight him again. Then it's out to Corner Brook and Port aux Basques to continue the battle with Satan!"

"Way to go, buddy! Keep pushing the bastard west all the way up to Canada," said the Doc.

### Doc Neil at Train Station

Doc Neil goes to the Railway Station in St. John's to catch a train to Clarenville. "What time does the half past five train leave?" Doc asks the station clerk.

"Five-thirty," replies the clerk.

"Well, the dockyard clock says its 25 past five, the lumber yard clock is showing 27 minutes past five and your station clock outside shows its 32 minutes past. Now you tell me, what do I go by," asked Doc.

"You can go by any clock you like, Doc, but you can't go by train 'cause it's gone!" answered the clerk.

### Hamlet at the Casino

During its early years, the Casino Theatre featured vaudeville acts and local on-stage productions. At a performance of Hamlet by a local group, the actor playing Hamlet was having problems with his part, and the audience began booing him. Eventually, the actor stopped his performance and walked to centre stage where he complained to the audience, "Ladies and Gentlemen, if you're not happy with the show, don't blame the actors. We didn't write this shit!"

## Fortune Harbour made History

The following story was told by Joey Smallwood on his famous Barrelman radio show, years before he became Premier of Newfoundland.

Ronald Murray was a native of Fortune Harbour, Notre Dame Bay. A good many years ago, his great-grandfather went up to St. John's on business one summer. He came by the coastal boat, and when the boat came into the narrows of St. John's, he was greatly surprised to see the Captain on the bridge put something up to his mouth, and shout through it to somebody on the wharf that they were approaching. What surprised the great-grandfather was the loudness with which the skipper could talk. Of course, it was a megaphone the skipper was using, and he was delighted. He pleaded with the Captain of the ship to sell him this megaphone, and after awhile, the Captain agreed and the bargain was made. The old time Fortune Harbour man passed over the money and received the megaphone. He could hardly wait to finish his business in the capital, according to the story told by Ronald Murray himself, and start off home again with his precious megaphone. 'Twas a happy day when, at last, he landed in Fortune Harbour and walked proudly up to his house to show his wife the megaphone, and explain its use. He put the gadget carefully away and waited for the opportunity he had in mind from the moment he'd first seen it used in St. John's. That was squid jiggin' time. At last it came around, and getting out the megaphone, he climbed up a ladder to the roof of his house, and putting it to his mouth, roared out to Uncle Joe on the squid-jiggin' ground, "Uncle Joey! Hi, Uncle Joey! Any sign of squid yet?" Getting no answer, he shouted again, "Uncle Joey? Are there any squid jigged yet?" Uncle Joey had heard the first time, he heard him plainly, every word and wondered, what in thunder was making it possible for the man on shore to talk so loud. He figured he must have a bellows fixed up to his mouth somehow to give him more wind to roar louder. He shouted back in reply, but, of course, the man on shore couldn't hear a word. Realizing why he couldn't hear Uncle Joey's reply, Mr. Murray's great-grandfather called a young fellow, gave him the megaphone, and told him to row out to Uncle Joey with it. Out on the grounds, Uncle Joey put the megaphone to his mouth and roared back the answer, and then sent the megaphone ashore for a reply. Thus it was many years ago that the first broadcasting system was born in Newfoundland.

## Vaudeville Quips and Stories

I spend a lot of money on food because my family won't eat anything else.

\* \* \*

Ned's got a big problem. He got to feed seven small mouths and listen to one big one.

\* \* \*

Fagan is so thin, his back pockets are in his other pants.

\* \* \*

Angus is so stupid, he didn't know he was twelve until he was thirteen.

\* \* \*

Teacher: Your essay about your cat is the same as your sister's!

Pupil: Yes, it's the same cat.

## Poor Rower

During the mid-1920s, the BIS Crew found themselves on the horns of a dilemma. There was a weak man in the boat, but the other crew members didn't have the heart to tell him. As Regatta Day drew near, the coxswain decided that he would take the bull by the horns and confront the weak man. He told the others, "We'll have to throw sentiment aside and tell Jim that he'll have to be replaced."

The next day at practice, the cox called Jim aside and reluctantly said, "I don't know if you know it, but there's a weak man in the boat, and...." That's as far as he got. Jim replied excitedly, "That's alright," bubbling over with enthusiasm and confidence, "tell you what you'll do...you just add a few more inches to my oar, and I'll make up for the weak man!"

## Honourable Soaking

During the 1920s it was traditional for a few committee members to be assigned the task of firing the gun to start each race. Each member would usually take every third or fourth race so that everyone could have some time to enjoy the day. On one occasion at about 5 p.m., one of the starters had been having a drop of the "national" and fell asleep. Suddenly someone shouted, "Time for the next race!" The judge's boat was already at the head of the pond, but our friend, hearing the shout, jumped to his feet and ran madly down the wharf and jumped into what he thought was the boat, but there was no boat there. Friends pulled the embarrassed fellow from the pond and the race went ahead on schedule without him.

## The Cow

During one of the Regattas of the late thirties, a new coxswain on the Pond was very keen, but lacking in experience. He looked the part of a coxswain, being short and light, but he had very little knowledge of the technique of taking a crew down the Pond and back.

Several days before the races, he asked a fellow cox for some advice. The old-timer asked, "What buoy are you on?" On being told the stake and buoy, the adviser said, "It's quite simple. After you get below the boathouse, steer for the white house at the foot of the Pond. That's right in line with the buoy you've drawn. You can't go wrong." The newcomer was delighted and expressed his thanks to the veteran.

On Regatta Day, his crew got off to a great start and he was in the race all the way. Mindful of his instructions, he kept his eyes fixed on the white house and paid little attention to getting to his buoy.

Unfortunately, when he got to the foot of the Pond, he discovered to his horror that he was heading for the wrong buoy. In his excitement, he had picked as his guiding point, not the white house but a white cow which was grazing in the field at the foot of the Lake. His crew came in last and our hero nearly ended up in Belvedere Cemetery.

### Not Judas

In old St. John's, an Irish priest delivered a number of stinging sermons criticizing the British, which prompted his Bishop to give him a stern warning to change his topic immediately. He complied, although reluctantly to the request, and for a month never mentioned the British. Then one Sunday, he could restrain himself no longer. He told his congregation he was going to tell the story of the Last Supper.

He said, "The good Lord told His disciples that one among them would betray Him. The venerable Peter asked, 'Is it I, Lord?'

"The Lord answered, 'It is not.' He asked the same question of John, James, Thomas, and they all received the same reply.

"Then Judas Iscariot arose slowly from his chair, looking shiftily around the room with his beady eyes, and asked, 'Blimey, I say, Guvnor, is it I?'"

### Without Malice

A young man, bruised and bleeding, staggered into the old lock-up behind the post office on George Street, and made a complaint to the desk sergeant that his mother-in-law had beaten him up. The officer asked, "Did your mother-in-law strike you with a malice and aforethought?"

"Naw, she hit me with a bucket and a broom handle," answered the man.

### Quoting the Bible

When Alice Walsh, a St. John's woman, gave birth to a child soon after the fire of 1892, she had a novel, but very inexpensive way of passing the good news on to her mother, who lived in Harbour Grace. She telegraphed the simple message:

"Isaiah 9:6"

This referred to a section in the Bible which reads, "For unto us a child is born, unto us a son is given." There would have been no problem had her mother, who was familiar with the Bible, had received the telegraph. She didn't! Her father received the message and read it. When his wife returned home from visiting friends, he enthusiastically informed her, "Mary! Mary! Alice had a baby and it weighs nine pounds six ounces. But, hell, I don't know why she called him Isaiah!"

### Dickie McGee

Dickie McGee was entertaining some of his street friends with his detective stories on the steps of the old post office on Water Street west. Doc Neil, whose behavior was always unpredictable, joined the group. In his best Sherlock Holmes imitation, McGee interrupted his story and addressed Doc Neil. "I see you are wearing your winter underwear, Doc."

"Amazing, McGee, and how did you ever figure that out?" asked Doc Neil.

"Elementary, my friend," said McGee, "when you stepped into the middle of the crowd, I took note that you were not wearing your trousers!"

### The Pandemic Flu of 1918

The Spanish Flu, as the Pandemic flu was known, took its toll in Newfoundland and Labrador during 1918 and 1919. In its latter stages the following poem appeared in the *Evening Telegram*:

*The "Flu"*
*When your back is broke and your eyes are blurred*
*And your shin-bones knock and your tongue is furred,*
*And your tonsils squeak and your hair gets dry,*

*And you're doggone sure you're going to die,*
*But you're scared you won't and afraid you will,*
*Just drag to bed and have your chill*
*And pray the Lord to see you through,*
*For you've got the flu, boy. You've got the flu.*

*When your toes curl up and your belt goes flat,*
*And you're twice as mean as a Thomas cat,*
*And life is a long and dismal curse,*
*And your food all tastes like a hard-boiled hearse,*
*When your lattice aches and your head's a buzz,*
*And nothing is as ever it was,*
*Here are my sad regrets to you –*
*You've got the flu, boy. You've got the flu.*

*What is it like this Spanish flu?*
*Ask me, brothers, for I've been through.*
*It is by misery, out of despair,*
*It pulls your teeth and curls your hair,*
*It thins your blood and breaks your bones,*
*And fills your craw with moans and groans,*
*And sometimes, maybe, you get well.*
*Some call it "Flu" – I call it HELL!*

(author unknown)

## The Proposed Union of St. Pierre and Newfoundland

Following WWI, serious thought was given by Britain to push for the annexation of St. Pierre to Newfoundland. Behind the idea was the concern that the island of St. Pierre might fall into the hands of an unfriendly country. A James McQuinn from New Brunswick wrote a letter to the *Evening Telegram* criticizing the idea and knocking the "Irish."

The following letter entitled *"Fee! Foo! Fum!"* was written in response to McQuinn and was signed by – Sunny Jim.

So James McQuinn, you're sore afraid
The Irish will be coming o'er,
To take St. Pierre and make of her
A terror to our native shore?

That bold Sinn Feiners armed with all
of Prussian ingenuity
Will make a grand Heligorland
Of our French neighbours property.

Oh! What a dreadful thing 'twould be
To see the standard of Sinn Fein
Float o'er that Isle where oft we've drank
To Liberty in pure champagne!

I pondered on this fearful threat,
My ponders e'er were filled with doubt –
And while I sought a rhyming word
I dozed, and this I dozed about.

I saw a strange bright banner wave
Upon the horizon of morn
I knew it, I have sought it long –
The signal of a race new-born.

And all the dream – ships of the years,
The centuries – went floating by,
And many a minstrel's voice to me
Rang o'er the morning wave in joy.

They bid me join the song they sang,
A warlike number 'twas and clear.
I saw them "clear the decks" – and then
I woke in trembling for St. Pierre!

*Beware! The Fenian man-of-war*
*Is on the main and I've no doubt,*
*McQuinn, thou knight of shaky knees*
*She'll catch you if you don't watch out.*

## Upholding Court Dignity

The dignity of a court must be maintained at all times, but it was difficult to maintain during a court hearing at the St. John's Court House in 1925. A very dignified judge, who was a little shortsighted, was presiding over a case which had attracted more than the usual number of spectators. During the hearing he noticed a man in the courtroom apparently wearing a cap. He rapped for order and said that all men must remove their hats. The case went on, but when he glanced back into the court a few minutes later, he again thought he saw the cap. Calling the sheriff, he ordered him to "remove that man's cap," pointing him out.

The sheriff investigated and found that what was bothering the judge was an unusually bushy head of hair. The sheriff explained the situation to the judge whose face reddened as he resumed the hearing. Learned counsel had a very difficult time restraining their laughter.

## Piano Player

Old Johnny Power from Lazy Bank was sitting with friends on the verandah of their house on Leslie Street in St. John's. His friend's daughter was playing the piano inside the house when the mother commented, "It's beautiful, isn't it?"

"What did you say?" asked Johnny.

"I said the music, it's beautiful isn't it?" replied the mother.

"Sorry Mary, I can't hear a word you've said with the noise from that god damn piano!" answered Johnny.

## Taking things literally!

A family of six comprised of husband, wife, and four children decided to attend a talking film at the Nickel Theatre. With tickets in hand, they stood outside the theatre entrance waiting for the usher to show them to their seats. The usher approached the father and asked, "How many do you have?"

He replied, "Oh, just the four. There were seven but we lost three during the Spanish Flu."

Lost for words, the usher simply showed them to six vacant seats.

### What Was She Doing?

A certain Water Street coal and oil merchant had an engagement with a client, leaving Mrs. O'Reilley, his new charwoman in possession of his office. Before going out he said to her, "Now, Mrs. O'Reilley, if you hear the bell attached to that little box in the corner ring, just go to the rubber mouthpiece and say, "Hello! Who's there?" then wait for a reply."

He had not been gone long before the bell rang, "Whir-r-r-r-r!" The woman ran to the phone and shouted, "Hello! Who are yer?"

"I'm Steve Clark over at Job's Wharf," was the reply. "I've got a lot of oil for you, and I need to send it on at once instead of tomorrow, so please, be ready to receive it."

After a while the merchant returned and saw the charwoman holding an empty bucket to the phone's mouthpiece.

"Whatever are you doing here with that pail?" he asked.

"Well, sir, " she replied, "just as soon as ye was gone, a man howled through that new-fangled tube that he was going to send some oil on to ye at once, but I didn't see a barrel or a basin handy for it, so I'm holding this pail to save the grease from dirtying the clean-washed floor."

### Walsh's Bread Advertisement

The following advertisement for Walsh's Bread appeared in the *Evening Telegram* during June 1930.

> *If all the bread baked at Walsh's Bakery in a year were put in a straight line end to end, it would extend completely across the country from Cape Spear to Cape Ray. At that*

*rate, it would take just eighty years to put a girdle of bread around the whole earth. All of which proves nothing. But if you were to take a loaf of Walsh's Bread and a print of fresh butter, you could sit down to the finest meal you have enjoyed for years.*

### Wilson's Meat Market

E. Fowler of Topsail, a veteran of World War I, won a five dollar gold piece in 1921 for his verses promoting Wilson's Certified Bacon. It was published in the *Evening Telegram*, December 23, 1921.

When the bells were softly pealing
In the tower o'er the way,
Long and loud the pigs were squealing
Somewhere in the U.S.A
One by one as they were taken,
Not a word to them was said,
Since they knew delicious bacon must be made from pigs well fed.

Crowds were working in that factory
Everybody wore a smile.
Right well they knew that Wilson's Bacon
They were making all the while.
In the stores the clerks were bushed,
For the news had lately come,
It was put upon the market
Everybody wanted some
Delicious bacon every crumb.

Back home again they quickly hurried
And soon the bacon it was fried.
Certainly after tea was over
One and all were satisfied.
Never did they taste such bacon as that Wilson's Certified.

– December 23, 1931

### Cigarettes Can Cause Insanity

The *Daily News* on August 3, 1905 reported on an unusual court case with a strange outcome. Louise Kinsella of St. John's died after consuming carbolic acid. An inquest was held to determine what had happened. The jury, after hearing the facts, determined that Kinsella's death had been caused by cigarette smoking. They claimed that the deceased was a chain smoker, and this excessive smoking caused her to become insane and this insanity caused her to commit suicide by drinking carbolic acid. The inquest jury recommended a better enforcement of the law regulating the sale of cigarettes.

### Tried to Steal Fowlers Hens

During the 1930s, Paddy Fowler of Cappahayden was upset when someone began stealing his hens. Paddy decided to set a trap to catch the thieves. The next night, he and his brother-in-law Tom Cahill hid in the shed which was used as a hen house. After they had been waiting a short time, a storm blew up and the shed started swaying in the breeze. After two hours of waiting, Tom Cahill, fed up, announced that he was going home, saying, "They'll not be here tonight, Paddy."

Tom stepped out of the shed and found himself on a motortruck moving slowly along the road. The hen-thieves had struck again and were stealing the hen house with all that was in it.

### Andy

*If any other comes for Mayor,*
*I'm for Andy.*
*It's only right, I should declare*
*I'm for Andy.*
*He's given all his time, 'tis true,*
*He's given all his brains, not few,*
*So that is why I'm telling you,*
*I'm for Andy.*

*He always was the poor man's friend,*
*I'm for Andy.*
*For them his work is without end,*
*I'm for Andy.*
*What other man can say the same?*
*What other man played such a game?*
*Honoured forever will be his name,*
*I'm for Andy.*

*His father, too, was Councillor,*
*I'm for Andy.*
*John Carnell knew what things were for,*
*I'm for Andy.*
*So from the father to the son,*
*The city's work is handed on,*
*And all admit it is well done,*
*I'm for Andy.*

*Make no mistake, on polling day*
*I'm for Andy,*
*I want each citizen to say,*
*I'm for Andy.*
*Once more he'll head the blooming poll,*
*Once more for him the votes will roll,*
*He well deserves the, "pon my soul,"*
*I'm for Andy.*

*So let us all wish him good luck,*
*I'm for Andy.*
*And Mrs. Carnell helps the Mayor*
*In Church and State she's always there,*
*Together they're a dandy pair,*
*I'm for Andy.*

– by "Gawb"

The above poem was written during October 1937 and published in the *Evening Telegram*.

Mayor Andy Carnell was among the most popular politicians of old St. John's and was often referred to as Newfoundland's LaGuarda, a comparison to the popular Mayor of New York City.

### Wanted a Doctor

Kate, who operated a boarding house on Gower Street, phoned her family doctor and asked if he could make a home visit because her husband was too sick to leave the house. The doctor told her not to worry, he only thinks he's sick.

Next day, Kate called the same doctor and asked, "Can you come to the house now doctor, my husband thinks he's dead."

### The Hunter

Paddy, who was from St. John's, was visiting his cousin Ambrose on the Southern Shore. One day, Ambrose suggested that Paddy take his dogs and go out and do some hunting. Paddy thought it was a good idea, borrowed the dogs and gun from Ambrose and went out on the barrens. When he came back, Ambrose asked how he made out.

"Great boy," answered Paddy. "Have you got any more dogs?"

### Beauty and the Bishop

Bessie was a well-built, beautiful woman with long blond hair, but she had the vocabulary of a longshoreman. At a reception held to honour the visit to Harbour Grace of the Roman Catholic Bishop from St. John's, Bessie found herself seated next to the Bishop. When the meal started, the Bishop turned to Bessie and commented, "My dear, you remind me of an old Rembrandt."

Bessie, with raised eyebrows faced the Bishop and answered, "Well you ain't so goddamned hot yourself!"

### Telegraph Costs

Bill, a tight-fisted fellow from Trinity, had to send a telegraph to relatives telling them that Uncle George had died at the General

Hospital. The Telegraph clerk told him it would cost one dollar for ten words. Bill wired, "Uncle George died Monday. No pain. Seven, eight, nine, ten."

### The Fortune Harbour Seaman

During the 1890s, a fellow from Fortune Habour named Paddy Hamilton, who believed in ghosts, joined the British Navy and found himself serving on a man-of-war. He asked his mates, "Is this ship haunted?"

"She's as full of ghosts as a churchyard. They are ten thousand strong between decks every night," replied the cook.

This so terrified Paddy that whenever he turned into his hammock, he pulled his blanket over his head and face so that from his knees downwards he was always naked and cold. After a month at sea, the captain asked him, "Well, Paddy, how do you like the man-of-war?"

"Very well, Sir," Paddy whined, "but your purser's a terrible rogue!"

"How so?" says the captain.

"Why he serves out blankets that don't fit a man. Do you know, sir, they are all too long at the top, and too short at the bottom? They cover my head and ears, but my feet are always perished with the cold. I have cut several pieces off the top and sewed them to the bottom, but the devil a bit, ya can't get it any longer," explained Paddy.

### "Chewin' the Rag"

– *Evening Telegram*, March 26, 1907 p6

(Mister Mick Cashin refers to Sir Michael Cashin, one of Newfoundland's Prime Ministers.)

*What is the matter with "Mister Mick" Cashin?*
*Why does his "babbling" tongue ever wag?*
*Why does he gabble in such a wild fashion*
*With his silly babble when "chewin' the rag?"*
*It is because his bait is not selling,*

*That's why he's flying the old Tory flag.*
*His bosom they say for his country is swelling,*
*When "Mister Mick" Cashin is "chewin' the rag."*
*"Mister Mick" Cashin, the Tories you're proud of them,*
*But the "people" are sick of your bluster and brag,*
*You are the "laughing stock" for the whole crowd of them,*
*"Mister Mick" Cashin, when "chewin' the rag."*

– Native

## Judge Flannery's Court

In the early part of the twentieth century, the court of Judge Flannery drew many daily spectators because one didn't know what to expect. Not being able to raise bail wasn't a problem.

The following item was taken from the daily *Evening Telegram's* column "Meeting out Justice, Before Judge Flannery." March 1907.

> *Richard Lawlor, 28, fisherman, failed to put in an appearance when called this forenoon, charged with being drunk while in charge of a horse and slide. Lawlor had, as the old folks say, a most curious cargo when arrested. The slide contained a barrel of flour, a keg of molasses, a sack of bran, a flask of gin and a bottle of Friar's Balsam. He left behind him, at the Police Station, a barrel of flour and a sack of bran, as a deposit for his appearance which he will forfeit if he doesn't put in an appearance.*

In the case of one Mickey Reddy from the Southern Shore, who was visiting St. John's for the first time, Judge Flannery showed compassion. The circumstances of his case were as follows. Mickey went drinking at various liquor establishments along Water Street. When he was ready to leave town, he couldn't remember where he left his horse. He tried to claim a horse that was not his and got into an argument with its owner. Constable Stapleton arrived on the scene and took Mickey to the lock-up.

Next morning, Mickey appeared in Flannery's court. After reading out the charges against Mickey, Judge Flannery leaned over and said, "I see it's your first time in the city."

"'Tis that your honour," replied Mickey.

"Tell me," Mr. Reddy, " what do you think of it?" asked Flannery.

"It's wonderful grand, your honour, but there's something that puzzles me," answered Reddy.

"What is that," asked Flannery.

"Well, your honour, with all the gin mills, whiskey wells, and shebeens on Water Street, why did they call it Water Street?" replied Mickey.

After telling Mickey he could send him to the Forest Road Hotel (HMP), he said he didn't want to discourage him from coming back to the city. He charged him fifty cents for housing his horse and wagon over night in the police stable, and bid him farewell.

During April 1907, the following item appeared in the *Evening Telegram* "Judge Flannery court news":

> *Yesterday, a resident of Rossiter's Lane, who shipped for the good of the voyage and his master's interest, the latter being the firm of H&T Burke, of St. Jacques, was arrested under warrant for failing to keep to his promises. He evidently preferred the mossy banks of "Lazy Bank" (Pleasant Street) to the Grand Banks of Newfoundland. His Honour remanded him until the steamer is ready to take him to St. Jacques to prosecute the fishery.*

In the same week the Justice Column reported:

> *A fifty-eight year old cooper, address The Poor House, Sudbury Street, finds no place like the Poor House after all. He stood to the bar this forenoon, and when asked what brought him there, remarked, "Your Worship, I was only*

*drunk and singin' a song. I drank notin' since Christmas."*

*"You may go," said Judge Flannery.*

*"I'm off to the Poor House," said the man, and the crowd tittered as the poor fellow glided noiselessly through the court house door.*

Above: John Brown's store at Cross Roads.

Right: J.T. Martin Undertaker.

St. John's waterfront.

Rawlins Cross, St. John's.

*All photos courtesy of City of St. John's Archives*

# Chapter 5

# Wit and Humour
# 1725 to 1890

Although Newfoundland had a small population in the eighteenth and nineteenth centuries, there was no shortage of humour. Stories for this chapter have come from a wide range of archival materials including: ancient wills, church records, political records, personal diaries, military records, Regatta records, old publications, newspapers, medical records, tombstones, obituaries, stories handed down from generation to generation and even ancient maps.

## Proof Cabot Landed at St. John's

In nineteenth century Newfoundland, people often referred to a site at the head of St. John's Harbour as proof that John Cabot landed at St. John's in 1497. A chart of St. John's Harbour, surveyed in 1798 by Francis Owen, Master of the HMS *Agincourt*, shows a site just outside the north side of the Harbour and a little north of the Battery, which the map identifies as "Wash Ball Rocks."

According to the oral history from old St. John's, the place was named by John Cabot after the Matthew stopped there before entering St. John's Harbour to allow the crew to bathe and wash their private parts.

## Maybe, "You can take it with ya!"

A William Abbott from Bonavista, Newfoundland made a rare bequest in his last will and testament. Abbott, a bachelor, passed away around 1850 and left an estate involving a house, property, boat, and land. His will was registered with the court and is now preserved at the Newfoundland Archives. The first bequest in the will read, "I give my soul into the hands of almighty God and my body to the earth by way of Christian burial, and upon resurrection, I shall receive the same again by the power of the Almighty."[1] All other possessions of Mr. Abbott went to his nephew. On judgement day, no doubt, he has a written notarized legal document to bring his body and soul together once more.

## The Governor and Friends

The following story of violence has a humorous side to it because of the people involved and where it took place. John Collins, commander of the military garrison in St. John's in 1729, was a victim of an amazing personal assault. This happened before Newfoundland had her first regularly appointed Governor. John Collins, in his position of commander of the military, was assumed to be the Governor in 1729. Collins was known as a pret-

---

1. During the mid-nineteenth century it was not uncommon for devout Christians to include similar bequests in their wills.

ty rough and abrasive character. These qualities eventually got him in serious trouble with the ladies of St. John's.

The circumstances leading up to the assault began at a party at his residence which was attended by the leading residents of St. John's along with their wives. Among the guests were Reverend John Jackson, Church of England minister, and his wife. During the evening, the Governor became intoxicated and made a comment that shocked the gathering. The comment was to the effect that there wasn't a lady in all Newfoundland. An awkward silence greeted the remark. Reverend Jackson asked, "Do you mean not one good woman?"

"No, not one!" roared Governor Collins.

"And do you include my wife?" the Reverend asked.

"I think the same of your wife that I do of all women," Governor Collins replied.

This comment provoked the women present to physically attack Collins. This attack was described in the newspaper, the *Newfoundlander*:

> Not able to bear this gross aspersion upon their honour, the women, with one accord, attacked the Governor who, being overpowered by their fury, could not defend his face from being disfigured by their nails, nor his clothes from being torn off his back, and what was much worse, one of the women cut the hamstring of his leg with a knife, which rendered him a cripple his whole life after.

### Music Lovers?

A big band was performing a concert of classical music at the old Benevolent Irish Society Hall. Most of the prominent people of St. John's were present. At times, the music would be thunderous and crashing and then trail into silence. At one of those near-silent sequences in the hall, the loud voice of a woman could be heard telling a friend, "I fry my toutons in fat back."

### Death by Beer

Two St. John's citizens lost their lives in a peculiar manner on October 28, 1845. John Grant and Thomas Walker were employees of Bennett's Brewery on Sudbury Street when they fell into the fermenting vat and drowned.

Although this is a true story, it did spark a humorous comment or two. One of these claimed that Tom Walker managed to get out of the vat twice to go to the bathroom.

### The Card Player

A source of great recreation in early nineteenth century Newfoundland was cards, and the most popular card game was "Five and Forty." H. M. Mosdell, in his book of notable events, included the following anecdote about a well-known lady card player in old St. John's:

> This lady awoke from a comfortable snooze in the middle of the parson's sermon, and hearing a voice that had been much in evidence the night before in her own house, called out loudly, "Hearts are trumps!" Of course, the effect was electric.

### Invisible Petticoats

In 1807, the *Royal Gazette*, then in its first year of publication, published the following advertisement for a company doing business in St. John's:

> **For Sale**, on the most reasonable terms by Follett, Hoyles & Co. – Liverpool Salt, Bread, Butter & Just imported – a few "INVISIBLE PETTICOATS."

In describing the episode, H. M. Mosdell in "What Year Was That?" wrote, "It is too obvious that the title was compromising, besides it was ridiculous on the face of it, and no wonder the girls laughed. Invisible petticoats!"

The rhymster (not identified) caught hold of the fun, and in the next *Gazette* appeared the following lines:

'To Sylvia,' I remarked, "Against the storm
No petticoat protects your gentle form:
The thinness of your dress is really risible.'
She said, and summoned up a serious air:
'Your optics are deceived, I've on a pair
'Which must elude your eyes – they are invisible!'

### British Sailors Take out Ad
From the *Newfoundlander*, November 1945:

*In St. John's in 1807* there were thirty-three licensed saloons and taverns, not to speak of shebeens[2], of which there were many. In those times the only policemen in St. John's were the saloon-keepers. When a man was sold a license to keep a saloon, he had to agree to perform police duty in the city without wages or any other type of payment. Those were the times when the old seaport was frequented by literally hundreds of foreign vessels every summer, and perhaps the most eagerly welcomed, from a social standpoint, were the British warships with their sailors and handsome young officers. Well, here's an advertisement which sent a wave of excitement among the fair sex and brought about a lot of gossip among both sexes:

Some naval officers lately arrived in St. John's being anxious to enter into HOLY STATE OF MATRIMONY and not having any opportunity of making their wishes known to the Fair Ladies of this Island, (of whose beauty they have the highest opinion) but by a communication of this kind, sincerely trust that any Lady whose inclinations may lead her to wish for a partner for life, will address a line to A.Z., Post Office, to which the most faithful and prompt attention will be given as well as the secrecy which ought to be observed on this occasion. N.B. The ladies will please note, there is not a married officer on either of the ships in question.

---

2. A Shebeen is a place where alcohol is sold illegally.

## Martin the Cockatoo

Martin the Cockatoo was a character of old St. John's who died in a major fire on December 12, 1856 that destroyed fourteen homes on Water Street near Job's Long Bridge. Martin was once convicted in court of assaulting a shop owner on Water Street. The incident that led to the court appearance took place following a snowstorm. Martin the Cockatoo went door to door in the merchant area of Water Street looking for a hobble clearing snow from the sidewalk. At a store near the old Market House, he asked the owner, "Shall I shovel off the sidewalk?"

The store-owner thought to amuse himself at the Cockatoo's expense and replied, "No, I may need the sidewalk again, but you can shovel off the snow!"

The witty comment sparked some laughter among customers nearby and angered Martin the Cockatoo who struck the owner with his shovel. The man was not seriously injured, and the judge fined the Cockatoo one dollar, or five days in jail. The Cockatoo was able to pay the one dollar fine.

## Paddy the Foot

Paddy the Foot was a character of nineteenth century St. John's. He often made a nuisance of himself in the business establishments along Water Street. In just one day, Paddy the Foot was tossed out of O'Mara's Drugstore several times. Finally, Mr. O'Mara himself came out and forcibly ejected him. O'Mara had just turned his back when he was startled by a loud crash. He turned around quickly and saw that Paddy the Foot had burst through the door. When the police came to take him, he casually explained that it was an accident. He said when Mr. O'Mara tossed him out into the street, he struck a wall of fog that bounced him back into the store. The judge sentenced him to five days in jail.

## Martin the Cockatoo at Italian Wake

During the 1850s, an Italian family named Lo Cicero had settled in St. John's and was living on Water Street west near the residence of Martin the Cockatoo. When Tony Lo Cicero Sr. passed away, The Cockatoo visited the family home where the old Italian was being waked. He later told his friend Paddy the Foot, "These Italians have a strange custom. They put a twenty-dollar gold piece in the hands of the corpse before they bury him."

"I heard of that custom," explained Paddy the Foot. "The money is to pay the man's way across the River Jordan."

"Well, I hope old Tony can swim," said The Cockatoo, "I got the gold piece in me pocket!"

## Paddy the Foot Shows Anger

A fellow from Water Street west was being tried in court at St. John's for assaulting his wife and mother-in-law with a hammer. The Judge asked the accused, "You said that on St. Patrick's Day you were involved in a dispute with your wife, is that correct?"

"It is, your honour," answered the witness.

"And during that dispute you hit your wife with a hammer and knocked her unconscious, is that correct?" asked the Judge.

"'T'is true, your honour," responded the witness.

"You're a bastard!" shouted Paddy the Foot from his seat in back of the courtroom.

Paddy's comment was ignored by the court, and the Judge continued his questioning of the witness. "After knocking your poor wife unconscious, you then turned your attention to your mother-in-law and hit her twice with your hammer, is that also correct?" asked the Judge.

"You are correct again," said the witness.

"You are nothing but a dirty, rotten, filthy bastard!" shouted Paddy once more.

"Bailiff, bring that man to me!" the Judge ordered as he pointed to Paddy the Foot.

Paddy approached the bench and told the Judge, "Your honour, that man is my next door neighbour and on St. Patrick's Day I asked him for a loan of his hammer and he said he didn't have one. He's nothing but a lying bastard."

## Wedding Caused Gossip

The marriage of Dr. Henry Thompson to Ann James of Broad Cove on Friday, April 1, 1842, had tongues wagging in old St. John's. The unusual marriage took place at Blackhead and the ceremony was performed by Reverend Sutcliffe. What made the marriage unusual was that Dr. Thompson was thirty-three years old while his bride was seventy-three years old. This true event was reported in the *Public Ledger* in April 1842 with the following comment, "Joy seized her withered veins and one bright gleam of nuptial life shone on her setting sun."[3]

## The Hearse and the Piano

In the late 1850s, the Spanish Consul in St. John's was a Spaniard named Don Uriarte. Tom Mullock, brother of Roman Catholic Bishop Mullock, was a known practical joker around town. Tom operated a brokerage business in which he purchased and sold all sorts of things. On this occasion, the Spanish Consul asked Tom Mullock to find a good piano for him. A few weeks later, Tom succeeded in finding a suitable piano. However, he couldn't resist turning its delivery to the home of Don Uriarte into a bit of fun. He sent the piano to the Spanish Consul's residence through the streets of St. John's carried on a funeral hearse. It was a sight that attracted widespread attention, and a procession of the curious formed behind the hearse to see where it was going.

The funeral hearse stopped in front of the Consul's home and the driver went and knocked on the door. Don Uriarte was astonished and angered by the scene that greeted him. The presence of a crowd of grinning spectators added fuel to his Latin fire, and when he sighted Mullock standing beside the hearse, he demanded angrily, "What for, Mr. Mullock, you bring me my piano on ze hearse, eh? What for?"

In his slow Irish drawl, Tom Mullock answered, "Well, Don Uriarte, I got the piano for you at a very fine price, and as it was

---

3. The bride died on June 20, 1845 and Dr. Thompson married Ann Janes of Broad Cove on November 1, 1845. The Dr. Died on February 12, 1868.

such a bad bargain, I thought a hearse was the most appropriate way to deliver it to you!"

## Old Punishment

In old St. John's, three sailors, an Englishman, Irishman and a native-born Newfoundlander were convicted in Court for causing a brawl and destroying property in a public house on Water Street. After finding the trio guilty, the judge sentenced each of them to thirty lashes on the bare back. First to receive the whipping was the Englishman. He was asked if he wanted anything on his back before the punishment was administered. He asked to have his back rubbed with a warm oil. This was done, and the whipping was carried out. The man was taken away in agony. Next came the Irishman, who, when asked what he wanted on his back, replied, "Nothing, absolutely nothing. I am a true Irishman, and will take my punishment like a man. The Newfoundlander's turn came and when he was asked what he wanted on his back he replied, "The Irishman!"

## The Duel at Quidi Vidi

In the early part of the nineteenth century, two Irish fishermen living in St. John's confronted each other in a duel that was fought on the banks of Quidi Vidi Lake. The dispute is said to have been over a stolen bottle of whiskey. Mike had stored away a bottle on his fishing boat, and after it disappeared, blamed his friend Paddy for the theft. Paddy chose to defend his honour by challenging Mike to a duel, and Mike readily accepted.

Soon after dawn on the appointed day, Paddy and Mike, accompanied by their seconds,[4] faced off in a duel with pistols. No sooner had they taken their places when Mike noticed an inequality in the situation. Mike was stout, while Paddy was thin.

"Bejasus," Mike said, "I'm twice as big a target as he is, so I ought to stand twice as far away from him as he is from me!"

"Be aisy now," replied Rory, his second. "I'll soon put that

---

4. The role of a second in a duel was to assist the duelist in preparing for the duel.

right." Taking a piece of chalk from his pocket, he drew two lines down the stout man's coat, leaving a space between them. Turning to Paddy he said, "Now fire away, ye spalpeen, and remember that any hits outside that chalk line don't count."

There were no casualties as a result of the duel, except for the black eye sported by Rory as he returned to his work station later that morning.

### Crime Item in 1886 Newspaper

*The trial at St. John's, Newfoundland of Carlos Zuzuarrugier for the murder of Stanislaus Caste by treacherously hacking off his head has been concluded, and the assassin sentenced to death. A few days before the perpetration of this terrible crime, the assassin was seeking about St. John's for suitable nails to crucify his mother.*

The Charlottetown Herald *is responsible for the above item of news. There is not the slightest excuse for this display of ignorance, since the facts of the case were telegraphed from St. Pierre to Halifax and New York and appeared in all the papers. Perhaps the editor of the* Herald *never reads his exchanges. Carlos Zuzuarrugier was a Spaniard who killed a man in the French settlement of St. Pierre and never was in St. John's.*

– The Evening Mercury,
St. John's, Newfoundland,
September 13, 1886

### Tombstones

Sometimes humour was found where it had not been intended. During the 1820s, a man named John Bedford was accidentally shot and his remains were buried at the Established Protestant Cemetery where the Anglican Cathedral is located today in St. John's. His tombstone read:

"This stone marks the resting place of John Bedford, accidentally shot, as a mark of affection by his brother."

Another tombstone at the Long's Hill Cemetery in St. John's read:

"Catherine Doyle expired after being ordered by her Doctor to a warmer climate."

On a tombstone somewhere in Notre Dame Bay erected by a widow in memory of her loving husband read:

"Rest in peace – until we meet again."

An epitaph at the old RC Cemetery on Long's Hill was painted onto a wooden headstone by someone unknown and left as a marker on the grave of a man who once served as a Bailiff. It read:

*Beneath this clay*
*Lies Paddy Day*
*The bailiff and the bum!*
*When he died,*
*The devil cried,*
*Come with me, Paddy, come.*

The following epitaph is said to have been in one of the ancient cemeteries in, or near St. John's:

*Here lies the body of Mary Jane,*
*Josiah was her husband's name.*
*She caught a cold in a shower of rain,*
*And that was how she Heaven did gain.*
*She suffered much for a very long while,*
*And is not buried here, but in the Straits of Belle Isle.*

The following epitaph was on a tombstone in the old General Cemetery at the corner of Duckworth Street and Church Hill in St. John's.

*Here lies I and my two daughters.*
*Kilt by drinking old bog waters.*
*If we had stuck to Epson salts,*
*We shouldn't be lying in these here vaults.*

From the old Renews Graveyard:

*Don't attempt to climb a tree,*
*For that's what caused the death of me.*

Another:

*Here lies Michael Ollerhead,*
*Who died from cold caught in his head.*
*It brought on fever and rhumatiz,*
*Which ended me – for here I is!*

At Fortune Harbour:

*Here lies John Hinchley*
*whose mother and father were*
*drowned in their passage*
*from old Ireland.*
*Had they both lived they would*
*have been buried here.*

## The Price of Coal

Old Maher operated a coal yard on Water Street during the 1800s. One day, while frustrated with the efforts of a new man he had hired a few weeks before, Maher addressed him, "You, George, are beyond any doubt the biggest idiot I have ever had the misfortune to employ in my coal yard. I can't teach you a single thing!"

George: Well, Mr. Maher, I larnt one thing from ya since I came to work.

Maher: And just what would that be?

George: That seventeen hundred pounds makes a ton.

The records show that George did not lose his job.

### Bishop Mullock and the Hymn Singer

During a visit to a northern Conception Bay village, Bishop Mullock was housed at the home of the McCarthy family who were devout Catholics. He was awakened early his first morning there by the soft tones of a soprano voice singing, *Nearer, My God, to Thee*. The Bishop meditated on the piety which Mrs. McCarthy must possess to enable her to start her daily work in such a beautiful frame of mind.

During breakfast, he told her how pleased he was to hear her sing, "...a marvelous hymn with such a beautiful voice."

Mrs. McCarthy responded, "Oh, that's the hymn I boil the eggs by. Three verses for soft and five for hard."

### No Converting Ambrose

The good Bishop Mullock was asked to go to a Southern Shore community to try and convert a particularly vicious old fisherman named Ambrose, who was notorious for his godlessness. Ambrose was so stubborn and hardheaded that he resisted every argument and piece of wisdom put forward by Bishop Mullock.

"Ambrose," the Bishop said, "are you not touched by the story of the Lord dying on the cross to save your soul?"

"Are you trying to tell me that the Lord died to save me, when he never seen me, nor knowed me?" asked Ambrose.

By this time, the good Bishop was running out of patience and trying not to show it. He replied, "Ambrose, it was a darn sight easier for the Lord to die for you just because He never saw you, than if He knew you as well as the rest of us."

## The Value of Prayer

On a visit to Renews, Bishop Mullock gave a sermon on the value of prayer and how to pray to ask God for blessings. His sermon was inspiring and many were nodding their heads in agreement. When he finished, he asked if anyone felt inspired enough to stand and say a prayer asking for blessings for the community.

Paddy Kenny stood up and said that he would make such a prayer. He bowed his head in meditation for a minute or so, then began his prayer, "Lord, send the poor unfortunates of this community such nourishment as we desperately need. Send us a wagon load of bread, a boatload of fish, a barrel of salt, Lord, and a barrel of pepper." Paddy hesitated a moment in contemplation, then resumed his prayer, "No, by thundering fish heads, Lord, that's too much pepper."

## Pass the Hat!

A replacement priest was sent to a small community in Conception Bay to fill in for the parish priest who had been hospitalized. Following the service, he passed around his hat for the purpose of taking up a collection. The hat was passed throughout the congregation and returned to the priest empty. The priest turned the hat upside down and shook it so that its emptiness would be known to all. He then raised his eyes to the ceiling and exclaimed with fervour, "I thank God that I got back my hat from this congregation."

## The Bee and the Parson

The parson of a small church near St. John's, while addressing students at Sunday School, was talking about the importance of controlling anger. He said, "You should never lose your tempers. You should never swear or get excited or angry. I never do." To illustrate, he said, "See that fly on my nose. A good many wicked men would get angry at the fly, but I don't. I never lose my temper. I simply say, 'Shoo fly! Go away fly! Get! Good Jasus, it's a God damn bee!'"

## Captain Arthur Jackman

One spring, in particular, there were two characters from St. John's on the trip to the seal hunt with Captain Jackman. One character, who was named Pat, was from the centre of St. John's and was very tall. The other, who was named Mick, was very short and was from Kilbride. There was no love lost between the two and Captain Jackman became well aware of it during the trip.

One day, when all hands were ordered by the Captain to go out on the ice and start the hunt, Pat fell in. Mick, who was nearest to him, should have hauled him out but made no move whatsoever to help. Pat managed to crawl and climb out of the cold water onto the ice.

Later, when all the men had returned aboard ship, Captain Jackman scolded Mick sternly, "What have you got to say for not helping Pat out of the water?"

In a flash, Mick answered, "Bejasus! Skipper, the man is so darned tall, I thought he was standing on the bottom!"

## Laziest Newfoundlander

The laziest man in nineteenth century Newfoundland was a fellow who lived near Trepassey named Poppy Power. The good people of the area had become tired of contributing to his support and there was much debate as to what to do with him. Finally, a group of fellas, after downing some homebrew, decided that if Poppy was never going to lift his bones again to support himself, then the proper place for him would be in the local cemetery.

They dragged a homemade coffin from a nearby shed and went to Poppy's little cabin where he lived alone. Poppy did not resist as they got him ready for burial and placed him inside the coffin. "He's too lazy to move," one frustrated man commented, as they lifted the coffin onto the makeshift hearse. The hearse was a ramshackle wagon dragged along by an old horse.

As the rather unusual cortege moved through Trepassey, curious residents asked, "Whose getting buried?"

"Poppy Power. He's too lazy to support himself, so we're going to bury him alive," answered the leader of the group.

"I'll give him a barrel of fish," said one man
"I'll give him a barrel too," another said.

Poppy slowly raised his head and asked, "Are the fish cleaned and salted?"

"No, Poppy, you'll have to clean and salt 'em yerself," replied a fisherman.

Gently laying his head back into the coffin, Poppy said, "Drive on, boys, drive on."

### The Politician

*When a hen lays eggs, with each*
*She is impelled to make a speech.*
*The self-same urge stirs human bones,*
*Whenever men lay cornerstones.*

### Outport Hospitality

Almost a century ago the Church of England rector at Hermitage in Hermitage Bay, Canon Bishop, decided to visit Bay D'Espoir, which was included in his mission. In a settlement in the bay, he became the guest of an old lady with whom, apparently, his predecessors had stayed. She was very hospitable and did all in her power to make him comfortable.

The Reverend was greatly surprised, however, the next morning to be awakened by someone tugging at the sheet on his bed. It was the old lady who had come into the room. She told him that she was going to get his breakfast and wanted the sheet for a tablecloth. About ten or fifteen minutes later, she came into the room again and took something from the foot of the bed. He asked her what it was?

"My bread," she explained, "I always put my bread at the foot of the parson's bed to rise."

The next morning he was awakened very early by the clucking of a hen. The old lady came into the room and said, "Don't be frightened, sir, my hen always lays in the foot of that bed, and she just laid an egg for your breakfast."

### The Reverend Fiddle

*A young Theologian named Fiddle,*
*Refused to accept his degree,*
*For, said he, t'is enough to be Fiddle,*
*Without being Fiddle D.D.*

### Tavern Signs

A sign hanging over the door at *The Traveller's Joy*, a tavern on Water Street in nineteenth century St. John's, depicted a sailor in a blue jacket and brass buttons with his right hand raised and beneath it the inscription, "I fight for all." A fisherman was depicted next to him with the inscription, "I pay for all."

At Peggy Rose's tavern at Twenty-Mile Pond was displayed the sign which read, "I've trusted often to my sorrow. Pay today and trust tomorrow."

### Old Advertisement

The following advertisement appeared in an issue of the *Newfoundland Gazette* in the 1850s.

> *WANTED – For a sober family, a man of light weight who fears the Lord, and can drive a pair of horses. He must occasionally wait at table, join in household prayer, look after the horses, and read a chapter in the Bible. He must (God willing) rise at seven in the morning, obey his master and mistress in all lawful commands. If he can dress hair, sing hymns and play at cribbage, the more agreeable. Wages: $75.00 a year.*

Another ad in the same newspaper, in 1880, read:

> *Blacksmith and barber's work done here; horse-shoeing and shaving; locks mended and hair curled; teeth drawing. Take note: my wife keeps school.*

## The Ugly Club

The following item appeared in the *Newfoundlander* newspaper, May 1946:

> *Probably one of the most unusual groups or clubs ever instituted in Newfoundland was that which started in St. John's in the early decades of the last century. This particular one was called the "Ugly Club," and the only qualification for membership in it was that a man had to be ugly and had to admit that he was ugly, in fact, he made this admission by applying for membership. By the time it was thoroughly organized and in full swing, it boasted of having the ugliest men in the city as members. They all gloried in their ugliness and despised good-looking men. It is recorded that despite their ugliness every one of the members of the Ugly Club became a married man eventually.*

## Kids Hopscotch Verse

The following is part of a verse kids sang when playing hopscotch in the late nineteenth century in St. John's.

*I have a dog as thin as a rail,*
*He's got fleas all over his tail;*
*Every time his tail goes flop,*
*The fleas on the bottom all hop, hop, hop.*

## The Cause of the Battle of Foxtrap

The Battle of Foxtrap refers to the rebellion by residents of that area in opposing the construction of the railroad through their community in 1881. The truth as to what inspired the anger is both amazing and funny. The construction of the Newfoundland Railway started in 1881 and by the end of summer, twenty miles of the grading had been completed and ten miles of rails had been laid. According to reports at the time, the inhabitants of the South Shore of Conception Bay strongly opposed the project. In an angry mood, a mob of people stoned the engineers, took away their instruments and drove them from their work.

Paul Carty, Inspector of Police, led eleven policemen from St. John's in an attempt to restore order. By the time they arrived, the mob had grown to five hundred men and women armed with guns and other weapons. The police, with bayonets drawn, quickly arrested the ringleaders and eventually order was restored.

For five days afterwards, the population from Indian Pond to Topsail was in an intense state of excitement. Newspapers reported, "All day long, they watched the engineers and the small posse of police and followed them from place to place. The people on the North Side of Conception Bay, Harbour Main and Holyrood, through the wise counsels of Reverend Jeremiah O'Donnell, did not offer any opposition to the building of the Railway."

When things had settled down, the true underlying reason for the discontent was learned. Prior to the opposition to the railway, several Irish settlers from Foxtrap visited a large Water Street store to pick up supplies and were told by the merchant owner that if the railway went through, a "toll gate" would be placed near the Long Bridge entering the city, and they would have to pay fifty cents to pass the "toll gate."

This little group of Irish immigrants rushed back to Foxtrap and went from neighbour to neighbour to tell them, in their Irish brogue, that if the Railway went through there would be a "tall goat" stationed at the Long John Bridge to stop them from going into St. John's, and they would have to pay a toll as well. So angered were they that a "tall goat" was going to be used to intimidate them, they took up arms to fight back!

### His Star of Hope

Outside it was snowing hard, and the teacher considered it her duty to warn her charges.

"Boys and girls should be very careful to avoid colds at this time," she said solemnly. "I had a darling little brother, only seven years old. One day, he went out in the snow with his new sled, and caught cold. Pneumonia set in, and in three days he was dead."

A hush fell upon the school room. Then a youngster in the back row stood up and asked, "Where's his sled?"

### Meant the Same One!

Edith, aged six, had just been told that she now had two little baby brothers – twins. She looked thoughtful, very thoughtful. At last, she spoke, "That's funny! Minnie and I both prayed for a baby brother, but we meant the same one."

### You're no Gentleman!

The Truant Officer made a surprise inspection of the school at St. Mary's. Had he known how well Miss Kelly, the school teacher, had all of her little boys and girls trained, he would have been on his guard. As it was, he eyed the youngsters while he rocked back and forth on his heels, and with his hands thrust deep in his pockets said, "Now children, I wonder if you know who I am?"

"You're no gentleman," was the reply, "or you wouldn't have your hands in your pockets!"

### Force of Example!

Jane was the elder, and at the party felt responsible for the behavior of her younger sister Madge. Therefore, it shocked her terribly when Madge proceeded to put a whole hard-boiled egg into her mouth. Straightway, Jane rose from her place at the table, walked over to the delinquent, and administered a sound whack on the ear.

Madge had a tearful tale to tell her mother when they got home, and mother remonstrated with Jane, "How could you, dear?" she asked. "And, in public, too!"

"Well," was the reply, "I just wanted to show them that even if Madge behaved so badly, I, at least, had been taught to have good manners.

### Stepmother

A little boy, attending school for the first time at Carbonear, was asked by his teacher to give his name. "Patrick Power," answered the boy.

"How old are you, Patrick?" asked the teacher.
"Dunno how old I am, Miss," stated Patrick.
"Well, when were you born?" asked the teacher.
"I wasn't born at all," said Patrick, "I got a stepmother."

## From Old Newspapers

During the 1830s, Newfoundland newspapers frequently printed the latest jokes from London. The best of these could end up in local concerts. One considered "immensely funny" was a story about Sir Thomas Moore. Susan Blake, a very close acquaintance, had pleaded with him to write what he felt would be an appropriate epitaph for her.

Sir Thomas came up with:

*Good Susan Blake in royal state*
*Arrived at last at Heaven's Gate.*

Susan was pleased. Some years later, and after having a falling out with her, he added these two lines:

*But Peter met her with a club*
*And knocked her back to Beelzebub!*

## Mrs. Murphy

"Ah, good morning Mrs. Murphy, and how is everything?"
"Sure, I'm havin' a wonderful time of it between me husband and the fire. If I keep me eye on one, the other is sure to go out."

## The Barking Dog

Two labourers were reporting to work at the home of the merchant, Mr. Duder, in St. John's. When the merchant's large barking dog came from behind the house, the two men stopped. "That's a fierce dog you got there, mister," commented Paddy, as he pointed to the dog.

"Oh, don't you know that a barking dog never bites?" said Mr. Duder.

"Oh, we know that, but what worries us is does the dog know it," replied Paddy.

## Better or Worse

Mrs. Kelly asks Mrs. Murphy, "How's your husband doing, Mae?" Mae answers, "Well, Kitty, it's like this. Sometimes he's better, and sometimes he's worse, but from the way he swears and yells and gets on when he's better, I think he's better when he's worse."

## Jokes from 1890s NL Newspapers

### *The Band*
"Will the band play anything I ask them to?"
"Absolutely, madam!"
"Well then, ask them to play chess!"

### *Good Memory*
Wife: "I hope you got a good memory for faces."
Husband: "Yes. Why?"
Wife: "I just broke your mirror."

### *Four Seasons*
Teacher: Johnny, can you name the four seasons?
Johnny: Salt, pepper, mustard and vinegar.

### *Tough Meat*
Paddy: This lamb is awful tough.
Gert: I'm sorry, the butcher said it was spring lamb.
Paddy: Well, I must be eating one of the springs.

## Scots Immigrants

Sandy McGregor operated a business on Water Street in 1820. He awoke one morning to find that his poor wife had passed away alongside him during the night. "Mary! Mary!" he shouted to the family servant.

"Yes, Mr. McGregor," Mary answered.

"Mary, ye need boil only one egg this morning!" said McGregor.

### Robber Caught

A Scots immigrant in St. John's during the 1890s was down on his luck and decided to rob a jewelry store. He tossed a brick through the window, filled his pockets with jewels and got away. He got caught by a police officer when he went back for the brick.

### A Nip in the Air

On the first day of winter, all the Scottish immigrants in St. John's walked around the city with their mouths open because there was a nip in the air.

Recipe for a Scotch Toddy: A glass of water and someone else's whiskey.

A Scotsman will drink...any given amount of whiskey.

### Treat the Budgie

McDougal to his wife: "'Tis ma birthday, Maggie. Hang the expense, give the budgie another seed."

### Mother Nature

"By God, Maggie, she gave you some dirty look!"

"Who gave me a dirty look?"

"Mother Nature."

### Loves Nature

"My, I really love nature," said the girl looking out over the ocean from Signal Hill.

"You've got real loyalty, after what nature did to you," said her boyfriend.

### Complete the Forms

"George, you forgot to fill in the blank!"

"What blank?"
"The one between your two ears!"

### Reason for Moving!

"Paddy O'Toole just moved in next door to me," said Mrs. Delaney to her friend Aggie.

"The same Paddy who used to live over the fish market on Water Street?" asked Aggie.

"The same one!" said Mrs. Delaney.

"I suppose he couldn't stand the smell of fish," observed Aggie.

"No, they couldn't stand the smell of him," said Mrs. Delaney.

### Great to see you again!

A Mr. Conroy, later to become Judge Conroy, was repeatedly interrupted by a heckler during a political rally in St. John's. The heckler shouted, "Do ya remember when yer father drove a donkey cart around St. John's?"

Conroy adjusted his glasses and fixed his glance on the heckler who was seated near the front row. He gazed thoughtfully, and then replied, "As a matter of fact, I had forgotten the cart, but I am grateful that the donkey is still alive. How have ya been all those years?"

### Replied in Verse

During the mid nineteenth century, Dunville, Placentia was called Power's Cove or, as it was pronounced then, Poore's Cove. Power's Cove was entered through a narrow gut called Power's Gut. Tom Power was the community leader and had a reputation for replying to questions in verse. One day an official census taker arrived at Mr. Power's door and asked Tom how many he had in his family?

Tom's reply was:

Pat, Mike and Tom,
Stephen, Maurice and John.
Bill and Ned are two that's dead,

Margaret, Theresa and Mary Ann,
There are seven boats inside my Gut,
And 70 sows within my Cove.

## "Casey Taking the Census"

"Casey Taking the Census" was one of more than one hundred and fifty songs written by the famous Bard of Prescott Street, Johnny Burke. Perhaps he was inspired by Tom Power who often spoke in verse. The following verses were taken from this once famous Burke song, which might have been sung to the tune of the "Kelligrews Soiree":

*I saw Long Bill, George Gill*
*And Tommy Frout from Nagle's Hill.*
*Jim Dinn, Dan Frim and Mary Francis Brown;*
*Kate Page, Joe Sage and Fanny Jones was in a rage,*
*The crowd I had to take them*
*When I went to do the town.*

*So I called on Betsy Shoestrings,*
*That's the woman lives next door,*
*I asked her about the family*
*And she told me twenty-four,*
*There is Fred and Ted and two*
*That's dead, Maria, Kate, May*
*And Andy on the Crusher*
*Earning thirty cents a day.*

*It takes a man of iron nerve*
*To do this job at all,*
*For dodging cups and tommy hawks*
*At every house you call;*
*I asked if all were of sound mind,*
*When in a rage she flew,*
*Get out said she you damn old fool*
*There's none as bad as you.*

### Johnny Burke

Johnny Burke and Richard McCoubrey, owner of the *Times* newspaper in St. John's, were next door neighbours on Prescott Street. Burke lived at number seventy-two, and McCoubrey lived at number seventy-four. One day, while Johnny was visiting McCoubrey, a customer of the *Times* knocked on the door. Johnny took it upon himself to answer. The customer, thinking Johnny worked with McCoubry, said, "I inserted an advertisement for my lost dog in the *Times* last week. Have you got any information for me? I offered a good reward."

"Sorry, the editor and reporters are all out looking for the dog," said Burke.

### Johnny Burke, Cub Reporter

In his younger days, Johnny Burke got a job as a reporter with the *Times*. After working there about one month, McCoubrey, the owner, complained to Burke that he left out names in his stories. Although a neighbour and friend of Burke, McCoubrey told him that if he neglected such details in the future, he would have to let him go. A few days later, John Casey's Barn was struck by lightning during a storm. Burke submitted the following story:

St. John's, Newfoundland, August 7 – A severe thunder and lightning storm struck St. John's last night. Lightning struck the wire fence enclosing the cattle on John Casey's Farm in the west end of St. John's. Three cows were killed. Their names were Elsie, Buttercup and Bossie.

### West End Boarding House

The warmth and comfort of the living room went to the head of George, the "star" boarder at a St. John's west end boarding house. George turned to Hilda, his landlady, and murmured gently, "Will you be my wife?"

Hilda stopped for a moment to consider. Then she said, "Well, you've been here four years now, George. You've never once grumbled at your food, or failed to pay your board promptly, and with no questions asked. No George, I'm sorry and I hate to refuse you, but you're too good a boarder to put on the free list." And that was that!

## The Politician at Renews

Daniel Greene, a St. John's man, was campaigning as a Liberal candidate in the Ferryland District during the 1893 Election. Mr. Greene arrived by boat in Renews and was on his own. He set out to find the home of his contact for the area, but was having trouble finding it. Carrying a suitcase, he walked along a road until he came to a farmhouse. He laid down his suitcase, opened the wired gate, picked up his suitcase, stepped onto the property, then closed the gate. He again laid down his suitcase and used his two hands to lock the gate with the wire. He walked a few hundred feet to the house and was greeted on the steps by Ned Conway. Greene introduced himself and said he was looking for a Mister Ambrose O'Neill whom he was told lived near Renews. Conway shook his head and told Greene, "I never heard of him. I'm sure there's no one in this area by that name."

Greene thanked him, then walked back to the gate, laid down his suitcase, removed the wire, picked up his suitcase, stepped outside, pulled the gate to, laid down his suitcase, and fixed the wire in place. He was just about to leave when Ned Conway called him to come back. Mr. Greene went through the entire process of opening the gate again and walked the few hundred feet to the house. When he arrived at the steps, Ned said, "I thought I'd tell ya. I asked me wife about that fella Ambrose O'Neill, and she never heard tell of him either."

## Suitable Regatta Motto

During the 1880s, the Regatta's motto was "Be temperate, genial and happy." The motto was part of an effort to discourage excessive drinking, and encourage people to enjoy the day at the races. During the Regatta of 1885, Paddy Murphy, having had far too much to drink, decided to swim across Quidi Vidi Lake. When Murphy, attired in coveralls and a salt and pepper hat, waded into the lake, the boats were just leaving the starting line. Constabulary Corporal Tim Dooley, in full uniform, dove in after Murphy and succeeded in dragging him back to shore. Nearby, spectators gave the Constable a round of applause. Looking at Murphy in a horizontal position on the ground, a lady who was close to him commented, "And the Regatta's Motto is 'Be temperate, genial and happy.'"

To which Dooley quipped, "Well, two out of three is not bad for Murphy."

## Toads, Rattlesnakes and Politicians

Toads and rattlesnakes were among the novelties at the 1883 Regatta. Newspaper editors took shots at each other whenever the opportunity arose. In that year, *The Evening Telegram*, reporting on the strange sideshow, used the opportunity to attack *The Evening Mercury* and the politicians of the day by stating:

> *The exhibition of Rattlesnakes and Nova Scotian toads for tomorrow on the Regatta Grounds at Quidi Vidi ought, of course, to embrace the reverend reptile of the Ting's* Evening Mercury *and the newly imported parasite who crawls about town in quest of editorial pablum for the editor-in-chief. Perhaps they will be there! Who knows? But after all, few persons, if any, will care to pay for the privilege of seeing a toad when almost every public office in the country contains one or more of these animals.*

## Short an Oarsman

A crew was short an oarsman for the St. John's Regatta. They were discussing their problem in a downtown tavern when they decided to attempt to recruit a rower from among the patrons. The coxswain approached a fellow from Bay Roberts who was standing nearby and asked, "Are you an oarsman?"

"Never been on an "oarse" in me life," answered the man from Bay Roberts.

### Better than St. John's

A St. John's man died and found himself in a strange place. From the people around him emerged a man, who while on earth had been his close friend and neighbour, and offered to show him around. After walking around and taking in the sights, the guide asked, "Well, how do you like it here?"

"Heaven is a damn site better than St. John's," answered the newly arrived St. John's man.

"Heaven! Who said we are in Heaven?" asked the guide.

### Potentially Shocking!

The Anglican Bishop for Newfoundland and his wife were returning home from a visit to London when their ship ran into a raging thunder and lightning storm. The Bishop's wife complained that the air was close in their room. In response, the Bishop opened the porthole and returned to bed. Amidst the roaring thunder and flashing of lightning, a wooden ball attached to a rope entered the room through the porthole and began bouncing around the room. Reluctantly, the Bishop got out of bed and knotted the string to the wall, then he returned to bed. With the ship rolling in the storm, the ball began to thump on the walls. Frustrated by the continuing noise problem caused by the ball, the Bishop got up and placed the ball beneath his pillow. Finally, the two managed to get back to sleep.

The next morning at breakfast, the Bishop told fellow guests of his overnight adventure with the storm, and the ball in his room. The story was greeted with laughter, but the Captain's reaction seemed to be excessive. He laughed loudest, and longest.

When his laughter subsided, the Captain said, "Why man! I mean your lordship, that ball you slept on hangs at the end of the ship's lightning conductor."

It was said that the Bishop turned pale.

### A Novel Name

A Harbour Grace woman had her firstborn son baptized as Alias Parsons. When a friend asked her why she choose Alias as the boy's first name, she replied, "It's a real popular name in St. John's. I saw it many times in the court records of the newspapers."

### Mother Surprised

When little Johnny returned from Sunday School, he shocked his mother by asking, "Mom, do I have any children?"

"I don't understand, Johnny, what do you mean?" his mother asked.

"The teacher was talking about our children, and our children's children, and it got me wondering if I had any children!" replied Johnny.

### Slick Lawyer

The following story was taken from *The Tribune*, a Newfoundland newspaper of the 1890s.

*A story is told of a St. John's lawyer some years ago who used an unusual expedient to get a client out of trouble. This client was charged with stealing a hog. When the man came to the lawyer's office to engage counsel, the lawyer took him into his private office.*

*"Now, if I take your case, you will have to be perfectly honest with me," the Lawyer explained. "Now tell me, did you steal this hog or not?"*

*"Well, yes sir, I did," the man admitted. "But I have a big family and no money and I sure was in need of meat!"*

*"That's all aright," the lawyer assured him. "You bring me half of that hog and I'll take your case."*

Then when the case was being tried, the lawyer obtained a verdict of not guilty by saying to the jury, "Gentlemen of the jury, this man did not get any more of that hog than I did!"

### News from *The Daily Tribune* – 1893

The following humorous, but true incidents were reported in *The Tribune* between May and August 1893:

### *Serio–Comic*

*A man came from Witless Bay on Thursday or Friday last who had been suffering for a long time with chronic indigestion. His intention was to go to the hospital to be treated. Not knowing the red-tapism (sic) required, he proceeded there, and meeting the doctor, of course, was refused admittance without the necessary order. He accordingly proceeded to the next person to get the order, and received one by mistake for the Poor House. Arriving at the Poor House, he went in, sat down and awaited the doctor. The invalid's appearance was very sickly, a long gray beard of fully six inches surrounded his sunken jaws and wan face, and his whole form was that of a patient of long suffering.*

Finally, the doctor arrived, and, as the story goes, took little or no notice of the patient, but shortly after went out again. Next came two policemen in a carriage, and enticed the poor man away, telling him they would take him for a drive, and all the other blarney required to get a lunatic quietly along.

*Finally, he was forced into the carriage and conveyed to the Lunatic Asylum where he was dealt with in a preliminary manner by the keepers, who shaved off his whiskers, cut his hair, and gave him the required bath. The family and friends of the man, hearing what had happened, hastened through the red-tapism (sic) that finally set him at liberty again. The poor man, finding himself free once more, remarked that he would rather die of indigestion than ever come to St. John's again to be cured, and if he had been kept in the Lunatic Asylum twelve hours longer, he would have gone mad.*

### A Touch of Shakespeare

The following advertisement for Columbia Tobacco appeared in *The Evening Telegram* on July 29, 1901:

*To be or not to be, that is the question? Whether it is nobler for a man to suffer the pangs of a scalding tongue, or use Columbia Tobacco, and by its sweet fragrance revere it. Columbia is the purest of black tobacco.*

### The Old Lunatic Asylum

Late one night at the old Lunatic Asylum in St. John's, a patient shouted, "I am Bonny Prince Charles!"

"How do you know?" asks a patient in the next room.

"God told me!" replies the first patient.

A voice from another room shouted, "I certainly did not!"

### Political Dirty Tricks

In the Newfoundland election of 1892, the Conservatives (Reform Party) under Sir James Winter were accused of using dirty tricks and giving out liquor to obtain votes. Among the candidates for Winter were Alfred Morine in Bonavista and Henry Mott in Burin. Following the election, a local poet wrote the following verse:

*Morine, Mott and Winter, three haters of gin,*
*Went forth "for to" capture the votes of Burin.*
*Said Winter to Mott, "As St. Peter's is handy,*
*You might nip across for a drop of good brandy.*
*I'm persuaded such seasoned old voters as these*
*The gentle persuasion of Temp'rance won't please.*
*To win the political battle I've come*
*And to win it – I'm certain – THERE'S NOTHING LIKE RUM."*

### Scold Your Wife

*If you wake up feeling bad,*
*Scold your wife.*
*If the weather makes you sad,*
*Scold your wife.*
*If your collar button slides,*
*Into some dark nook and hides,*

*As you move with angry strides,*
*Scold your wife.*

*If your tea is cold or flat,*
*Scold your wife.*
*If your chop has too much fat,*
*Scold your wife.*
*If you chance to get your sleeve,*
*In the butter do not heave*
*Soft sighs or in silence grieve.*
*Scold your wife.*

*If your hat has gone astray,*
*Scold your wife.*
*If you're late upon the way,*
*Scold your wife.*
*If the day brings any loss,*
*If you fail to please the boss,*
*Journey homeward, feeling cross,*
*Scold your wife.*

*Never mind what ills she bears,*
*Scold your wife.*
*Add your own to all her cares*
*Scold your wife.*
*That's the way to get along,*
*She is weak and you are strong,*
*Every time a thing goes wrong,*
*Scold your wife.*

— author unknown

## Bury the Dog

Paddy Cole's dog died and he borrowed his friend Ambrose's pick and shovel to dig a hole to bury it. After some time had passed, Ambrose went out to see how Paddy was doing. He was puzzled to see that Paddy had dug three holes.

"Paddy, why in God's name did you dig three holes to bury one dog?" asked Ambrose.

"Bejasus, Ambrose, the first two weren't deep enough," answered Paddy.

## Paddy Fowler

A fellow named Paddy Fowler from the Southern Shore used to visit St. John's every Saturday with a wagon full of vegetables, which he sold door to door in the city. He'd always stop at Casey's Saloon for refreshments before starting on the long journey home. On one such visit to Casey's, Paddy came out of the saloon to find that his horse and wagon had disappeared. He returned to the bar and told Casey to pour him another beer. Then he pounded his fist on the bar and roared, "Me harse and wagon is not where I left it. By the lard Jasus and all that's holy, if it's not back where I left it by the time I finish this beer, the same thing that happened last week up at Bay Bulls is going to happen here!" He struck the bar with his fist again for emphasis. His warning was received with silence and then a shuffling of feet as some men left the bar. Paddy finished his beer and as he turned to leave, he said in a loud voice, "Be-Jasus, the harse better be there!"

It was! His angry warning had worked. A fellow from Mundy Pond asked Paddy, "Tell me, sir, what happened at Bay Bulls last week?"

"Be-Jasus I had to walk home," replied Paddy.

## The Dump on the old South Side Hill

Johnny Burke wrote this song which was sung to the tune of "When you and I were young, Maggie". It refers to the old time dump on South Side Hills in St. John's.

*As I sit all alone by the fire, Maggie,*
*Strange fancies my mind often fill,*
*So I said I'd strike off a few bars, Maggie,*
*On that Dump near the old South Side Hill.*

*There, a new brand of oaths on the chart, Maggie,*
*And profanity the air often fill,*
*For the stink pots of China are mild, Maggie,*
*With that dump on the old South Side Hill.*

*Chorus:*
*For the perfume is there night and day, Maggie,*
*While iron bound noses it would fill,*
*And burnt rags get no show in the fight, Maggie*
*With that dump on the old South Side Hill.*

*Oh the stench from the night carts are mild, Maggie,*
*While some times they open out bad,*
*And the odour is not what you like, Maggie,*
*From the guns of a red iron clad;*
*But that dump on the hills takes the bun, Maggie,*
*It's a terrible sight for to see,*
*All the neighbors are now up in arms, Maggie,*
*Along with our local J. P.*

### Judge Prowse's Wisdom

The Newfoundland historian Judge D.W. Prowse visited Fortune Bay during the height of the rebellion against the Bait Act. The principal conspirator against the Crown on this issue was a man described by Prowse as, "...a willy Italian whom we will call Goldoni."

Prowse dropped in at Goldoni's store and listened as Goldoni argued in the presence of a crowded store, "The whole thing is the work of St. John's merchants, and Queen Victoria has no part in making the law and she is opposed to it."

Prowse considered how best to answer the argument. He recalled, "Some of my audience were Protestants, but the bulk of the company were Catholics." When Goldoni finished and the applause died down, Prowse took centre floor.

In describing the incident, he later wrote:

*Taking a half crown from my pocket, I asked, whose is this image and superscription, but the Queen's? Look at this Act, read the inscription. Can you believe for one moment that Queen Victoria would allow her name to be put to an Act like this without her consent? You see it is in her own name. Now, my friends, which will you confide in, a trusted servant of the Queen like your humble servant, or a blasted Italian whose country men are trying to murder our Holy Father the Pope?*

Unfortunately, Prowse's wisdom did not prevail, and to settle the dispute the Judge later returned at night with the soldiers and arrested the Italian and his supporters.

Jack Fitzgerald was born and educated in St. John's, Newfoundland. During his career he has been a journalist, a feature writer and political columnist with the St. John's *Daily News*; a reporter and public affairs writer with CJON and VOCM News Services; editor of the *Newfoundland Herald* and the *Newfoundland Chronicle*. During the last years of the Smallwood administration, he was assistant director of Public Relations with the Government of Newfoundland and Labrador. He has also worked as Assistance Officer with the Department of Social Services. Jack Fitzgerald also hosted a regular radio program featuring off-beat Newfoundland stories on radio station VOFM.

As well as writing about unusual happenings relating to Newfoundland and Newfoundlanders, Fitzgerald has also authored a series of Newfoundland crime and punishment stories as well as Newfoundland historical publications.